In the Country of Books

Commonplace Books and Other Readings

In the Country of Books

Commonplace Books and Other Readings

Richard Katzev PhD

Matador
9 De Montfort Mews
Leicester LE1 7FW, UK
Tel: (+44) 116 255 9311 / 9312
Email: books@troubador.co.uk
Web: www.troubador.co.uk/matador

ISBN 978-1848760-615

Typeset in 12pt Sabon by Troubador Publishing Ltd, Leicester, UK

Matador is an imprint of Troubador Publishing Ltd

In Memory of HHK & SPK

With deep gratitude

I live with books more than with people. Which is to say that I can easily do without people (there are days when I could easily do without myself), and that in the country of books where I dwell, the dead can count entirely as much as the living.
Adrienne Monnier

As I read the novel [Lawrence's Sons and Lovers] I sank into the world of Paul Morel. The text ignited a latent sense in me of the desirability of self-knowledge. There were other realities in life beside my own. I had not really thought about my life. I began to glimpse at the most elementary level fragments of my own reality. The novel calmed my turbulence, eased my restlessness and shame.
Paula Fox

Table of Contents

Preface

I talk about my books as if they were people, and I choose them the way I choose my friends: because somebody nice introduced us, because I like their looks, because the best of them turn out to be smart and funny and both surprising and inevitable at the same time.

Sara Nelson

In reading, friendship is suddenly brought back to its original purity. There is no false amiability with books. If we spend the evening with these friends, it is because we genuinely want to.[1]

Proust

Every now and then I find a work of literature that nearly takes command of my life, when my day is measured only by the time remaining before I can get back to it. Not long ago I went out of town for a few days to work on a project that was as remotely associated with literature as Newtonian physics. When I left, I was halfway through Azar Nafisi's *Reading Lolita in Tehran* and was eager to resume reading where I had left off.

1 Alain De Botton, *How Proust Can Change Your Life*, 1997. New York: Random House.

The book brought alive for me the meaning of literature for those who could only read and discuss it in hiding. Within an hour after returning home, I took up the book once again. A feeling of relief swept over me, an emotion I often feel in getting back to fiction. I am not sure what gives rise to this feeling. All I know is that when I am reading literature I fall into a mood, one of rumination, sometimes moody, sometimes elated, that makes the experience such an imperative. It is an effect not unlike the one Jonathan Franzen described in reading Alice Munro.

> *Reading Munro puts me in that state of quiet reflection in which I think about my own life: about the decisions I've made, the things I've done and haven't done, the kind of person I am, the prospect of death.*

With all the reading I've been doing lately, I have been led to wonder how and to what extent this experience has influenced my life. I first started thinking about this question in mulling over the many years I've been reading *The New Yorker*. It was about 50 years ago that I first began reading it in a fairly regular fashion. Not every issue to be sure and not every article each week either, but a goodly number of both. More recently, I've had the time to read each issue more carefully, some of which have been rather exceptional. Those I read thoroughly from cover to cover.

How have these reading experiences affected me? Have they changed me at all? In the beginning I looked into the research that has been done on the effects of reading periodicals, hoping, in my naïve way, to learn that the topic was a well-researched one. But no, it had not been investigated. At least, I failed to find a single serious piece of research on the topic.

Nor, in my case, do I have any idea how to answer that question. I do know I find it a great pleasure to read the magazine each week and that more often than not there is an article or short story that I save in order to think further about and follow up with further reading. And I know that a great many other individuals are life-long readers of the magazine and that it means as much to them as it does to me. But what difference has it made in their lives?

Absent research on the matter, I turned to the larger question of the effects of reading literature in general. I had better luck here, but not a great deal, as I could only find a few empirical studies of this question. I thought I had better dig deeper into the issue both personally and in terms of what other critics and investigators have written about the topic. This volume represents the results of this inquiry.

Reading great works of literature is not one I want to forget. So from the beginning of my reading days, I have been recording the notable passages that I come across in the books and periodicals I read. My collection of these passages has grown to well over three hundred pages during the almost thirty years since I have been adding to it. The attempt to analyze this collection and determine the meaning of its foremost themes is the first subject I take up.

In most critical discussions of literature, the experience of the reader is virtually ignored, as literary scholars tend to dwell on the meaning of the text from various theoretical or cultural frameworks. Instead, in this book I focus on the experience of the readers, how literature enters their lives, and possibly changes them. I have done so by describing my own literary experiences and have also introduced research findings that, in my view, help to clarify the issues I'm considering.

Many dedicated readers have played an important role in the evolution of this book, particularly the first section on the commonplace book tradition. I owe a special debt to each one: to Lauren Gale Albert for introducing me to the practice of keeping commonplace books and for her careful reading of an early draft of the material; to Olivia Dresher for her meticulous editing and innumerable ideas that have helped me throughout my work on this project.

I am grateful to Kim Greenwood for his insights and world-record modeling of commonplacing. Thanks to George Herrick for informing me about his scholarly research on commonplace books and to Jennifer Allen of the Oregon Council of Humanities for giving me the opportunity to investigate the organization's humanities reading program. I am extremely grateful to Audrey Borenstein for her encouragement and creative applications of the commonplace book tradition.

I also wish to thank all the readers who completed my survey on commonplace books and were willing to engage in follow-up exchanges on their experiences. Thank you Audrey Borenstein,

Patsy Cunningham, Olivia Dresher, Kim Greenwood, George Herrick, William Marchand, Sean McLachlan, Michael Newman, Michael Robertson, Dean Scaros, Philip Skelsey, George Strong, and David Willis.

Finally, I wish to acknowledge the tireless efforts of Juanita Rothman in guiding me through the publication process. Her continuing interest in my work has meant so much to me and I am most grateful for her friendship and support.

The contributions of each of these individuals have been a great source of inspiration. They have made working on this book a writer's dream.

[1] Alain De Botton, *How Proust Can Change Your Life*, 1997. New York: Random House.

Commonplace Books

Marks in the Margin

Time was when readers kept commonplace books. Whenever they came across a pithy passage, they copied it into a notebook under an appropriate heading...Reading and writing were therefore inseparable activities. They belonged to a continuous effort to make sense of things.
Robert Darnton

Whenever in my reading, occurs concerning this our fellow creature, I do never fail to set it down by way of commonplace.
Jonathan Swift

About twenty years ago I started to keep a record of some of the thoughts and ideas in the books that I had been reading. By then I had already turned 50 and while I had always been a reader, I don't know why I hadn't started before. I may have copied a few passages over the years, but I wrote slowly, often illegibly, and none of those written pages remain. What I do have, however, are over 300 pages of various extracts copied from the books and periodicals that I have read and then collected in what has become a rather huge spiral bound notebook. Following a long established tradition it is known as my Commonplace Book.

When I come across something notable that I have read, I put a little mark by it in the margin or enclose the relevant passage in parentheses. I invariably stop to think about it for a moment before adding the page number on which it appears to a list I keep on the inside back cover of the book or last page of whatever periodical I am reading. Once I've finished the material, I copy each of the passages that I've marked in a Word document on my computer.

I know some people feel differently about this, that the meaning of a passage can only be fully grasped by copying them by hand. But because I write so poorly the computer has made it possible for me to record these passages in a readable form with ease. I can't imagine having a volume of such length, or of any length for that matter, were it not for my laptop, nor that I would continue the practice so avidly without giving it a second thought.

Some of the books I read have a great many marked passages, others very few. I used to judge the quality of a book by the number of passages that I'd marked. Eventually I realized that was a mistake, since occasionally I come across a really worthwhile book in which I don't mark any passages. At the end of each year, I make a copy of the collected passages and add them to my ever-growing Commonplace Book.

Recently a friend wrote to me that she also keeps such a book, one that is not so much a record of her reading but rather of certain ideas that come up in the enormous number of books she reads. She believed the passages fell into some kind of pattern that she was trying to understand. My hunch is that she will spend a lifetime at this thankless task. She also said she would kill herself if she lost it. Well, it must be quite a treasure.

In the beginning my Commonplace Book was largely composed of quotations that struck me as worth recording for one reason or another. The first entry is from Samuel Coleridge: *Advice is like snow; the softer it falls...the deeper it sinks into the mind.* The idea has considerable appeal to me now, although I'm not sure why it did at the time I made note of it. Soon after there is one from William James: *Wisdom is learning what to overlook.* Again the notion has grown in meaning over the years.

Eventually the entries became longer. *When they ask me, as of late they frequently do, how I have for so many years continued an equal interest in medicine and the poem, I reply that they amount for me to nearly the same thing.* —William Carlos Williams. *At the breakfast table I always open the newspaper to the sports page first. The sports page records people's accomplishments. The front page has nothing but men's failures.* —George Plimpton.

Then I began to split apart the quotations from a miscellaneous collection of phrases and short extracts that I called Briefs. These could be anything from an amusing phrase or word, a short phrase from the *New York Times*, a periodical, or something I read on the web: *Eat! You need strength to worry.* —Jewish Fortune Cookie message. *The whole world seemed to have changed into a Robert Altman movie. Jarring and sour and crazy and colored in a palette that I believe drove my entire generation mildly insane.* —Michael Chabon.

Soon I begin to separate the Quotes and Briefs from the Passages that comprised the longer sections I began to copy from the books and periodicals that I was reading. For example, I copied several memorable passages from Ian McEwan's *Atonement*:

> *...the strangeness of the here and now, of what passed between people, the ordinary people that she knew, and what power one could have over the other, and how easy it was to get everything wrong, completely wrong.*

> *...nothing was ever as one imagined it.*

> *...truth was strange and deceptive, it had to be struggled for, against the flow of the everyday.*

> *The age of clear answers was over.*

> *Whatever humble nursing she did, and however well or hard she did it, whatever illumination in tutorial she had relinquished, or lifetime moment on a college law, she would never undo the damage. She was unforgivable.*

Each year my Commonplace Book consists of entries in each of these groups with the Passages by far the largest of the three sections. In 2004 I added thirty-seven pages of Passages and four pages of Briefs and since I entered only a few new quotations I did not print a new Quotes section that year. By way of comparison, in 1996, the first year that I began to distinguish the three types of entries, there were eleven pages of Passages, four of Briefs, and two of Quotes. This difference can be attributed to the fact I now have far more time for reading than I did in the nineties when I was still actively engaged in teaching and research. Beginning in 2002 the number of Passages increased almost twofold compared to previous years. I have no idea why this occurred. There was also a further doubling during the next four years so that last year, 2005, I recorded fifty-five pages of Passages. I think these changes are due largely to the improving quality of the books I am reading now. After all, one can only read so many romance novels.

Reading serious literature takes time. To make the most of it a reader should be able to linger over the text for a while, pause to give it some thought, stop to mark a memorable passage, and perhaps revisit it before moving on. Ideally a reader should be free of the distractions of pressing work deadlines, household chores, or other responsibilities and be able to disengage from the onslaught of the media, telephone, and the Internet. These are the conditions of my life now. It is also true that I've taken a liking to the practice of commonplacing; it has become a habit as well as a commitment to maintain a record of the noteworthy ideas that I have found on the pages of the literary works that I've been fortunate enough to be able to read.

In a recent interview at Salon.com[1] James Salter asserted:

1 http://www.salon.com/books/int/2005/06/17/salter.html

"Sentences should not cause you to stop and admire them. They should be in the service of the page." That brought me to a halt and I proceeded to do the very thing Salter said I shouldn't. After pondering his claim for a bit, I began to wonder if I should give up the practice required to maintain my Commonplace Book. Am I missing the sheer power of the page by stopping to admire a sentence or make note of one from time to time? Have I lost sight of why I began copying extracts in the first place and the inherent benefits of the practice? These questions more or less answered themselves, for in stopping to consider Salter's claim I was thoroughly in the "service of the page." It was not the sentence *per se* that caused me to stop. Rather, I stopped because of the effect the sentence had on me and the way it led me to want to make special note of its meaning and consider, for a moment, the several questions it raised.

Recently I've begun to wonder what it would it be like if I stopped my commonplacing activity. Could I do that? Would my reading experience be any different? The questions are not unlike those a person might ask who wishes to change a very strong habit. In a word, it wouldn't be easy. Marking and then recording the memorable passages in the books I read has become central to my reading experience. I usually stop reading a book when it doesn't engage me in this fashion. And so to discontinue the practice of commonplacing would make reading a far less absorbing experience than it has become for me.

I suspect many readers make little marks in the books they read. It seems a natural thing to do. Yet only a few readers that I know keep a record of these passages. A few years ago I learned that the practice began in antiquity and that it achieved considerable prominence during the Renaissance. Yet I was completely unaware of the tradition at the time I started my own collection. The fact that I, along with other readers, keep a commonplace book without knowing about this centuries old practice suggests it reflects a rather fundamental feature of the reading experience.

Frankly, I am not at all sure why I began the practice in the first place. The passages must have stood out for one reason or another and I may have wanted to make a record of them in order to reread them sometime in the future. I think I also had dreams of doing some writing. I know I admired a great many writers and often wondered how they were able to write so well. In my naïve way, I must have imagined that if I studied their works carefully and copied portions of them often enough, I might one day be able to write like they did.

In thinking back to the origins of my Commonplace Book, I realize now I must have found something in the literature I was reading that was not only different but was also somehow more truthful, more discerning about what truly mattered in my life than what I was reading in psychology. I don't recall collecting passages in the academic books and journals I was reading. Yes, I took notes but those were for my lectures and classroom presentations and were never added to my Commonplace Book or preserved in special notebooks. I may have placed them in a file for the next time I taught the class but not because I found them memorable or otherwise worth saving because they were especially significant.

I also know that the reasons that led me to begin my Commonplace Book have been largely replaced by others now. Transcribing memorable passages from the books I read is how I become truly engaged with the book, engaged with the issues that are important to me at the time of my reading. The issues change over time, but there is always the great pleasure of making contact with them on the page and then recording those passages I have marked in order to read them once again as often and whenever I wish

Lately, I have begun to think of my Commonplace Book as a form of collecting; in my case, collecting ideas as well as clever or provocative expressions that stand apart from ordinary discourse and are, for that reason, worth preserving. In some cases they serve as a standard against which to judge my own attempts to write with some degree of clarity. Collecting ideas also has a number of distinct advantages compared to collecting most other objects—they cost next to nothing, they are easy to find, do not clutter up your closet, and don't require periodic repair or maintenance.

Overview
When I began this project I was hoping only to look more analytically at my own Commonplace Book. I thought of it as an exercise, a novel approach to gaining some insights about myself. I soon realized, however, that I was far from alone in keeping a collection of notable quotations. This brought me in contact with the tradition of commonplace books stretching back to antiquity, as well as the works of other authors who have either published their commonplace books or carried out historical

research on the topic. Indeed, when I first started to think about the practice of keeping commonplace books, I had no idea of its origins or of those philosophers, scholars, and theologians who copied their favorite quotations, poems, or sections of the manuscripts they read.[2] Nor did I have any idea why these individuals spent so much time at this task or how they intended to use the material once they had so diligently transcribed it. I've briefly reviewed this historical background in Chapter 2. It is not a well-known literature or very extensive one either.

I also decided to try to find out how widespread the practice of keeping commonplace books is today by surveying others who keep one. The results, some of which surprised me, are discussed in Chapter 3. The recent appearance of commonplace books on the Web was a totally unexpected outcome of my inquiry and Chapter 4 presents an overview of this phenomenon, one that may foreshadow the future direction that commonplace books will take. In Chapter 5, I describe the results of the qualitative analysis of my own Commonplace Book and in the concluding chapter I discuss some of the implications of my findings.

2   Since I had never intended to publish the material in my Commonplace Book, I
    neglected to record the author and source of each selection. This was espe-
    cially true for the Briefs. In addition, the Passages were not properly referenced
    with page numbers, and in the case of periodicals, the year of publication and
    volume number. It is too late now to try to remedy this situation with specific
    citations for the hundreds of the passages in my Commonplace Book. More
    importantly, where the passage appears matters far less to me than the idea it
    conveys or the way it is written. I apologize to those readers who might wish to
    know the exact source of a certain passage(s) that I refer to in this volume.
    However, I believe it should be possible to obtain this information for the ma-
    jority of Passages, where at least the author and book title are noted and for
    most of the Quotes by well-known authors.

Gathering Nectar

We should imitate bees and we should keep in separate compartments whatever we have collected from our diverse reading, for things conserved separately keep better. Then, diligently applying all the resources of our native talent, we should mingle all the various nectars we have tasted, and turn them into a single sweet substance, in such a way that, even if it is apparent where it originated, it appears quite different from what it was in its original state.
Seneca

Make your own Bible. Select and Collect all those words and sentences that in all your reading have been to you like the blast of trumpet out of Shakespeare, Seneca, Moses, John and Paul.
Emerson, *Journals* July 1836

I speak of the collected volume of passages that I have transcribed from the books I've read as a commonplace book. So does Andre Bernard who edits a "Commonplace Section" for each issue of the *American Scholar*. Bernard collects extracts from various authors who have written about a particular topic and simply lists them on two pages of this publication without commentary or analysis. For example, recent topics have included Loafing, Change, Failure, and Marriage. A somewhat similar collection also appears in each monthly issue of *THE SUN*, http://www.thesunmagazine.org, where it is referred to as Sunbeams. For example, the January 2006 issue presented two columns of passages related to misfortune, despair and dying, from a wide range of authors including Socrates, Henry Miller, Mario Cuomo, and Ann Landers.

Yet a collection of this sort is quite different than the way "commonplace book" is formally defined. For example, the Oxford English Dictionary defines it as:

> *A book in which 'commonplaces' or passages important for reference were collected, usually under general heads; hence, a book in which one records passages or matters to be especially remembered or referred to, with or without arrangement.*

My collection was never intended to be a reference book, nor have I organized the material under separate heads or topics. Yet that was the way commonplace books were originally conceived. The term "common place" can be traced to the Greeks who referred to the group of philosophical arguments and discussion topics used by statesman and orators as *koinoi topoi* (general points). The Romans translated the phrase as *communes loci* (general areas of discussion) that scholars and orators also drew upon in composition or speaking. According to Gilbert Highet "some tasteless fellow Englished the term into "commonplaces."[3] The sense in which the headings were "common" signifies their acceptance as the fundamental beliefs and moral principals of the times. It is ironic that in popular speech the term has come to mean something rather ordinary and unremarkable since there is clearly nothing the least bit ordinary or common in the commonplace books that stretch back to classical antiquity and the Renaissance.

According to Earle Havens, Aristotle referred to the collected passages as: "the principal tools of any logical and systematic interrogation of the truth or falsity of an opinion."[4] It is in this sense that commonplace books were originally considered to be organized sources of knowledge and practical wisdom. In Roman times Cicero carried on the tradition by drawing his commonplace material from the works of philosophers, orators, and poets and subsequently applied them in his public speaking and courtroom presentations.[5] In the Middle Ages Scholastic philosophers continued the practice but turned away from secular applications and substituted instead theological and religious words of wisdom as the materials for their commonplace books.

From all accounts the commonplace book tradition reached its peak of popularity during the Renaissance. This was associated with the revival of classical learning and the emergence of the

3 Gilbert Highet, *Uncommon Thoughts in a Common Place*, Horizon Magazine, Vol. IV, September 1961.
4 Earle Havens. *Commonplace Books: A History of Manuscripts and Printed Books from Antiquity to the Twentieth Century.* University Press of New England. 2001.
5 ibid.

humanistic critique of Scholasticism. Havens writes:

> *Renaissance humanists, teachers, and students were among the first to deliberately invoke the term "commonplace book" to describe collections of quotations organized for the express purpose of demonstrating the best moral wisdom and rhetorical felicity of ancient Greek and Latin authors.*

Erasmus was perhaps the most influential advocate of drawing upon classical learning in this fashion and formulated several different methods for organizing the material. He was also instrumental in promoting commonplace books as an important educational tool, particularly in guiding students to a more disciplined method of reading.

In *A New Method of Making Commonplace Books*, John Locke presented one of the most systematic methods of organizing commonplace entries. At the outset Locke laid out an index keyed to each letter of the alphabet, each of which was divided into five separate boxes corresponding to one of the five vowels. Table 1 depicts one page of his grid.

He explained his procedure this way:[6]

> *When I meet with any thing that I think fit to put into my Common-Place-Book, I first find a proper head. Suppose for example, that the Head be EPISTOLA, I*

6   John Locke, *A New Method of a Common-Place-Book*, 1706.

Table 1

448   *A new Method of a Common-Place-Book.*

look into the Index for the first Letter and the following Vowel which in this instance are E.I. If in the space marked E. there is any number, That directs me to the Page designed for words that begin with an E and whose first Vowel, after the initial Letter, is I. I must then write under the word EPISTOLA in that Page what I have to remark.

Locke did not begin with a pre-determined set of topics; instead he created them during the course of his readings. They included a broad array of themes, each in turn, followed by the passage he selected, and a comment of his own.

During the Renaissance commonplace books were developed for a wide range of disciplines including literature, law, philosophy, and science. But with the rise of science and the diminishing importance of proof by authority, the value of commonplace book collections declined fairly rapidly. This process was accelerated by the development of comprehensive encyclopedias as sources of reference during the Enlightenment. Havens summarizes evidence that fewer and fewer printed commonplace books appeared during the eighteenth century, "a period marked by greater public familiarity with other distinct forms of text compilation—verse anthologies, concordances, encyclopedias…"

Over the course of the next centuries, commonplace books continued to be published although their character changed significantly. Rather than sources of knowledge, they became more personal collections of literary extracts, occasionally followed by brief comments, but largely unorganized and highly idiosyncratic in subject matter. Insofar as the passages in these printed collections were gathered together under specific topics or themes, they still deviated significantly from the earlier forms of commonplace books that were structured and indexed in a rather systematic fashion. In a word, the nature of commonplace books evolved from a resource for argument and persuasion in antiquity, to a reference for knowledge and wisdom that flourished during the Renaissance, into its contemporary version of a personal collection of memorable literary quotations without any formal conceptual scheme.

Representative Commonplace Books

Several well-known writers, scholars, and statesmen have kept personal commonplace books; some have been published during their lifetime, while others only after they had died. Two of the most notable of the latter group were the commonplace books of John Milton and Thomas Jefferson. In a comprehensive examination of Milton's commonplace book, Ruth Mohl, notes that: "When it was discovered in 1874 it was stained with dampness and was bound in rough brown sheepskin..." and had no lettering to identify its author. Only after its contents were examined, including a letter written to Milton, was it identified as his.[7] Milton's commonplace book was organized by thematic indices or headings, such as Morality, Economy, and Literature. Mohl illustrates how Milton's collection provided a storehouse of facts for his political tracts and poetry.

The descendents of Thomas Jefferson withheld publication of his literary commonplace book until 1928.[8] It was one of the two notebooks he kept during the early part of his life; his second notebook dealt with governmental and political issues. His literary commonplace book was based on the work of philosophers and poets and is the earlier of the two. According to Douglas Wilson, who edited a 1988 edition of the work, Jefferson maintained it from the age of about fifteen to thirty and, because it is the most personal of the two, it provides a

7   Ruth Mohl. *John Milton and His Commonplace Book*, 1969. New York: Frederick Ungar Publishing Company.
8   Douglas L. Wilson (Ed.) *Jefferson's Literary Commonplace Book* 1989. New Jersey: Princeton University Press.

rare glimpse of Jefferson's formative years and the considerable influence of literature on "the contours of his mind." Many of the entries, written by Jefferson in their original Latin, Greek, or French, seem to have been chosen because of their philosophical and moral content.[9]

In noting some of the similarities between Jefferson's and Milton's commonplace books, Mohl suggests both men selected passages not only for their literary merit but also as "sources of inspiration and practical wisdom."[10] Later she concludes that like Milton's, Jefferson's literary commonplace book is alive with:

> *Themes of courage, self-reliance, freedom, equality, the necessity of wisdom combined with strength, and faith in God...along with those on the brevity of life, death and the fatal beauty of women. In them the personality of Jefferson is strikingly revealed—as if in his own words he was recording his philosophy of life.*

As with the commonplace books of Milton and Jefferson, E. M. Forster's was not discovered until after his death in 1970.[11] He began it in 1925, when he was already 46 years old—about the same age I was when I started my own collection. His initial

---

9   Wilson indicates that of the 407 entries, 339 are poetry, and 35 of the 45 authors quoted are poets. Homer, Horace, Pope, Milton, Shakespeare and Euripides are among the most frequently quoted.

10 Ruth Mohl. *John Milton and His Commonplace Book*, 1969. New York: Frederick Ungar Publishing Company.

11 E. M. Forster *Commonplace Book*, Edited by Philip Gardner, 1985. Stanford, California: Stanford University Press.

plan was to organize his selections by topics, but after his first three entries, Commonplaces, Isolation and Resentment, he abandoned this scheme because he "found it too preconceived and dictatorial." Forster's *Commonplace Book* combines literary passages with personal commentary, sometimes related to the passage, sometimes simply a reflection on another topic, so that in many respects it is both a commonplace book and personal journal. It unfolds cumulatively over time and is said by Gardner to provide a rare view of Forster's intellectual and emotional life. Gardner describes the growing sense of alienation that appears in the passages towards the end of his life and the increasing frequency of literary extracts and personal comments related to change, illness and death.[12]

In 1957 Charles P. Curtis, a professor of Government and Sociology at Harvard, published a delightful and somewhat distinctive commonplace book.[13] Each numbered entry begins with a quotation or aphorism drawn from his literary reading. It is then followed by Curtis' commentary in the manner that Erasmus had originally employed in the several editions of his *Adages*. Like Erasmus, some of Curtis' comments are relatively brief, while others are rather extensive. For example, the third entry poses an amusing question. "In a sense, one can never read

---

12 One of the last entries Forster writes: "The belief that I may live after my breath ceases and my body begins to smell never occurs to me—either in the simple form cherished by my ancestors, or in the difficult modern ecclesiastical form…I think of death as a permanent anaesthetic—to be reached amidst pain or fear if my luck is bad, and under perfect hospital conditions if the luck's good. In either case it finishes me off as a memoirist or an observer."

13 Charles P. Curtis. *A Commonplace Book*, 1957. New York: Simon and Schuster.

the book that the author originally wrote, and one can never read the same book twice." It is followed by Curtis' comment:

> *This is the last sentence of Edmund Wilson's preface to his The Triple Thinkers. ' Books are like rivers. "You cannot bathe in the same river twice, for the new waters are ever flowing in upon you," Heraclitus said.' Or are we readers the rivers? And books the countryside through which we flow?*

In contrast, the twenty-second entry quotes a short passage from Marlow's *The Jew of Malta*: "But that was in another country; and besides the wench is dead." This extract gives rise to a three page commentary on the mystery of how "words move me without my knowing why or how." The appeal of Curtis' commonplace book is the wonderful interplay he creates between literary passages and his attempt to achieve some understanding of the reasons he was drawn to them. A good many people keep a record of their favorite quotes, proverbs, or literary passages, but far fewer annotate them by reflecting on their meaning and personal relevance as Curtis did.

David Cecil is quite forthright in admitting this is the case for his commonplace book. In 1975 Cecil published *Library Looking Glass*[14], an anthology of literary passages with extensive annotations that is in many respects a commonplace book at its very best. The passages are drawn from well known

---

14 David Cecil. Library Looking-Glass: A Personal Anthology, 1975. London: Constable and Company.

literary works, they are provocative, and most are followed with critical comments that are both autobiographical and a pleasure to read. Cecil's volume is also distinctive in that the passages are arranged alphabetically beginning with Art and ending with Wordsworth, leaving blank X, Y, and Z.

Some of the letters have more than one topic, as in "C" with entries on Change of Key, Child in the House, Colour Sense, Comedy, Class System, Classics, Commitment, Complaints, Comparative, Conservation, Content, Contrasts, and Criticism. In addition, more often than not, several passages have been listed for each topic. For example, Cecil has listed nine separate poetry passages for Autumn, while English Landscape has eleven.

Cecil was an English aristocrat, literary scholar, and biographer who taught at Oxford for many years. In an amusing introduction to the volume Cecil takes issue with those who recoil from the practice of writing in printed books. He says it is really a compliment to its author saying "It treats him as a living man, with whom one wants, as it were, to converse." In an echo of my own practice, as well as those of most contemporary readers who keep a commonplace book, Cecil writes:

> ...when anything in the text has especially struck me,
> I have noted on the end-paper the number of the page
> where this has occurred. Sometimes my note simply
> indicated admiration...The passage referred to was
> beautiful or comical or well-written in ways that had

a peculiar appeal to my own taste, or it stated a view
which I found especially illuminating; or it stimulated
in me a fruitful train of thought.

In a *Library Looking Glass*, Cecil has assembled a selection of these passages and has usually added a comment suggesting why they have evoked his interest. Cecil admits that his reasons were largely personal and for this reason his anthology can be thought of as a "sort of self-portrait; myself, as mirrored in the looking-glass of my reading." While his volume may be autobiographical, because there is no temporal order to the alphabetical ordering of the topics, it is difficult to read through from beginning to end, as one would read a personal history. Instead, I prefer to dip into it from time to time and skip around from topic to topic in no particular order. Whenever I do this, I find the passages Cecil has selected and his thoughtful commentaries a continuing source of pleasure.

W. H. Auden also organized his commonplace book, *A Certain World*,[15] under thematic headings arranged in alphabetical order. So, for example, the first two are Accidie and Acronyms, while the last two are Word and Writing—apparently he could not come up with anything worthy of citation for X, Y, and Z. Auden does not comment on every entry, preferring instead to keep his own reflections, particularly those that might be viewed as autobiographical, "to a minimum and let others more learned, intelligent, imaginative and witty than I, speak for me."

---

15 W. H. Auden. *A Certain World: A Commonplace Book*, 1970. New York: The Viking Press.

Nevertheless, his intermittent annotations are far from impersonal. For example, before listing passages from Proust, Ruskin, Goethe and others in the section on Ageing, Auden writes:

> *I was both the youngest child and the youngest grandchild in my family. Being a fairly bright boy, I was generally the youngest in my school class. The result of this was that, until quite recently, I have always assumed that, in any gathering, I was the youngest person present....It is only in the last two or three years that I have begun to notice, to my surprise, that most of the people I see on the streets are younger than I. For the first time, too, though still in good health, I am almost able to believe that I shall die.*

What could be more autobiographical than that? And a few pages later, before quoting a poem, *Park Concert,* under the heading Bands, he recalls:

> *When I was young, brass-band concerts were a regular attraction in the public parks of cities. Am I mistaken in thinking that they have become rarities? All I know is that this poem fills me with nostalgia.*

And under his last heading, Writing, after citing several passages concerning this topic, he comments: "Most of what I know about the writing of poetry, or, at least, the kind I am interested in writing, I discovered long before I took an interest in poetry itself." He continues with a two-page recollection of various experiences that influenced his work as a poet.

In a review of *A Certain World*, Benjamin DeMott considers one of the questions that led me to look closely at my own commonplace book, namely what it might reveal about the underlying patterns of a person's life.[16] DeMott suggests one can learn a great deal about the kind of person Auden is from the entries in his commonplace book. He writes that aside from what we already know about him,

> *You make out too that he's not young, that he's often melancholy and self accusatory, that he finds life short. And you can assume only a little speculatively, that he lends excitement to the lives of his friends not alone through his writing...[and is] a rueful, deep, humorous, loving man.*

It would not be a stretch to conclude that Auden's comments in his commonplace book are a good deal more personal than he is willing to admit. So too, I imagine are the entries of the authors of most commonplace books.

16 Benjamin DeMott. Speaking of Books: Auden's Commonplace Book. *New York Times,* September 13, 1970.

What Other Readers Say

To collect is to sympathize with art. To make one's own commonplace book is a good way to become a thinker—perhaps even a poet.
Gilbert Highet

A commonplace book is what a provident poet cannot subsist without, for this proverbial reason, that "great wits have short memories:" and whereas, on the other hand, poets, being liars by profession, ought to have good memories; to reconcile these, a book of this sort, is in the nature of a supplemental memory, or a record of what occurs remarkable in every day's reading or conversation. There you enter not only your own original thoughts, (which, a hundred to one, are few and insignificant) but such of other men as you think fit to make your own, by entering them there.
Thomas Swift

Has the practice of keeping a personal commonplace book disappeared as some commentators claim?[17] Before conducting an informal survey on this subject, I knew of only one other

17 Benjamin DeMott. Speaking of Books: Auden's Commonplace Book. *New York Times*, September 13, 1970.

person who kept a written or typed record of passages they selected from the books they had read. Surely other serious readers keep a comparable record. However, it is all but impossible to know how many, let alone what form their collection takes. To try to get some evidence on this question I placed a Writer's Query[18] in two consecutive issues of the *New York Review of Books* and the *Times Literary Supplement*. I received thirteen replies—six from England and the United States and one from Canada. Eleven of these individuals completed the short survey shown in Table 2 about their commonplace book and two of them were kind enough to expand upon their comments during a series of subsequent e-mail exchanges.

All of them expressed a sincere attachment and, in some cases, a deep affection for their commonplace book and the central role it played in their reading experience. One person put it this way: "I see my Commonplace Book as a kind of treasure chest…[confessing] This is what I believe is true; *this* is what I find to be beautiful." Another said "I copy the best words I have found, the intelligence of my times, of all times…And I do so out of pleasure and gratitude, endlessly working to assimilate what has been given me, paying it the justice of concrete attention…"

On average these readers had been maintaining their commonplace books for thirty-five years with a range of from five to sixty-five years. This variation seems largely a function of

---

18 Writer seeks accounts of contemporary Commonplace Books—record or journal of memorable reading passages including its purpose and role in your reading experience. Brief Commonplace Book survey sent if requested. Send questions and comments in confidence to rkatzev@gmail.com

Table 2

Commonplace Survey

This survey is designed to learn about your commonplace book, what form it takes, and the role it plays in your reading experiences. Your answers will be of value to me as I try to gauge the nature and extent of commonplacing among contemporary readers. Your response will be kept strictly confidential. Please write me if you have any questions at rkatzev@gmail.com

1. For how many years have you kept a Commonplace Book?

2. In what form do you keep it—written notebook, typed pages, computer document?

3. Approximately what size is the page and how many pages have you collected to date?

4. What are your reasons for keeping a Commonplace Book?

5. What types of materials do you draw upon in selecting passages for your Commonplace Book? Check all that apply:

Fiction (novels & short stories)	Quotations
Non-fiction (essays & memoir)	Poems
Quotations	Periodicals
Others (please specify)	Newspapers

6. How often do you review previous entries?

7. Do you annotate the selections added to your Commonplace Book? If so, can you please describe your practice?

8. Have you organized or analyzed the contents of your Commonplace Book in any way? If so, please explain.

9. Do you have an electronic version of your Commonplace Book? Yes No

10. As part of my research, I will be performing a statistical analysis of a small number of Commonplace Books. Would you be willing to have yours included in this analysis with assurance of complete confidentially? If so, would you be able to transmit it by e-mail?

11. Please add any further comments about the role of your Commonplace Book in your reading experience.

Thank you so much for taking the time to complete this survey. I am very grateful for the information you have provided.

their age, with the majority, as far as I could tell, into their fifties and sixties. Several confirmed my hunch that they had not heard of the term "commonplace book" or been aware of the practice when they began their own. In a delightful confession, one academic described a visit by W. H. Auden to his campus. After introducing Auden to the audience that came to hear his lecture, he went on to say that he "took him to the airport where we drank many martinis. He started to talk about his commonplace book, and I realized that is what I was doing too. As you probably know, his is published and mine will not be. His should be published. Mine should not be."

One individual reported he had been keeping his commonplace book for "as long as I can remember." Another said she had been doing so on and off since she was a child. All but one kept their extracts in hand written notebooks or bound volumes and two reported they kept several of their quotations on index cards taped above their writing desk or tucked inside their desk blotter. One individual, keeping pace with the times, kept his initially (35 years ago) in a written notebook, then on typed pages, and since 1996 he has stored them electronically on his computer. He had also gone to the effort of retyping all his previous entries on the computer; he was the only individual who said their commonplace book was in this form.

While the majority of individuals reported they had accumulated anywhere from two hundred to three hundred pages in their commonplace book, one reported, to my astonishment, that he had "accumulated 23 volumes, 4,550 pages, which at an average of 230 words per page, comes out to 1,096,500 words." And that is only from the *books* he had read! It takes no account of the passages he had copied from magazines, periodicals, essays, etc. that constituted almost another half of his commonplace activities. The combined total of *both* collections was actually 36 volumes, 7,170 pages and 1,685,500 words! This surely has to be some kind of a world record, probably qualifying for entry in the Guinness Book of World Records. I learned that he had transcribed 80 pages from De Beauvoir's *The Second Sex* and 140 pages from Nietzsche's *Will to Power*. He also claimed he generally reads about five books each month. I can also assure you that I was not the least bit surprised when he reported that he was 13 years behind in transcribing passages in his commonplace volumes and that he was currently copying passages from the books he read in 1993. What an astonishing account!

The majority of respondents said they reviewed their entries occasionally, a few as often as three or four times a year. The individual who appeared to review them most often said she did so every few weeks "to look up words that chime in my memory, to refresh my recollection of the material, or simply to browse and savor and rediscover anew their beauties and their teachings."[19] "At odd moments," she continued, "I open the books or folders at random, or spread the pages out, close my eyes and lay the palm of my hand on the page and then lift it to look and see what is there for me at that moment."

19 Audrey Borenstein, author of *One Journal's Life: A Meditation on Journal-Keeping*, 2002. (Seattle, WA: Impassio Press) and other works of short fiction, poetry, and criticism.

Most readers said they entered the passages they selected one after the other, over time, without arranging them in any systematic fashion. However, three said they organized some of their selections by themes or heads following the procedure of the very first commonplace authors. One person reported he kept notes from books on the psychological nature of a footpath that subsequently proved useful to an architect who was designing sidewalks for a new community. He also confessed that for years he collected the last words of dying people.

Two others said they kept some of their passages in notebooks or files explicitly devoted to a single topic. For example, one individual maintained separate notebooks on a variety of topics including "offbeat" quotations on such subjects as peace, feminism, etc. Another said she kept a notebook on Judaica, although she had only entered one quotation in it, one that she had cherished. Its author is Hannah Senesh; "I feel I could not possibly live without writing, even if only for myself, in my diary…A thought that is not put on paper is as if it had never been born. I can only truly grasp a thought when I've expressed it in writing."

The practice of annotating the passages was rare with the majority saying they never did. Three indicated they did so occasionally by adding short comments to a passage in their commonplace book at various periods after they had made the original entry and three others said that occasionally they made a short note on the page of the book they are reading. Similarly, none of the individuals reported they had organized the passages in any fashion, although a few said they would like to one day. One person rebelled at the thought of analyzing her commonplace book. She wrote: "Organization and analysis would contravene the unique value of my commonplace books for me: it would blind me to...invisible lines of connection between ideas and things that appear to dwell in mutually exclusive realms."[20] Yet another reader wrote in defense of the practice: "Why do I do this? Is there some thread running through it all? Is there some thread running through my life?"

More than anything I wanted to know why individuals went to the effort of copying passages from the books they read. What motivated them to engage in this practice and how did they intend to use the collection they assembled? Three themes emerged in the responses I received to this question. Foremost among almost everyone's answer was the desire to *preserve* passages that stood out from the text by virtue of their truth, cleverness, or quality of the writing. As one reader put it, her commonplace book was a way of "snagging fleeting movements and preventing them from vanishing utterly, even a way of preserving a snapshot of one's own identity."

Their rationale was uniformly based on the limitations of recall, that a reader can barely remember a fraction of what they read. Keeping a commonplace book is a method for overcoming these limits and ensuring that the memorable passages they have taken the time to record will be recoverable at some later date to be reviewed and examined anew. One reader reported: "It adds an element of permanence to my reading experience which

i20 bid.

too often seems ephemeral given the volume of reading I do and the limitations of memory." In citing this important function of commonplace books, these readers were echoing the rationale long ago voiced by Francis Bacon:

There can hardly be anything more useful...than a sound help for the memory; that is a good and learned Digest of Common Places...I hold diligence and labour in the entry of commonplaces to be a matter of great use and support in studying...

A few individuals pointed out how this transformed their reading experience into a more critical, reflective process than it might otherwise be. Readers who keep a commonplace book may be more engaged with the text than those who don't. Rather than skimming lightly over the text, they often read more slowly, stopping from time to time to mark a passage, and to think about its significance for a moment or two. And by keeping a commonplace book they can repeat the same process when they review the passages they have transcribed. One individual referred to the experience as one of "self-involvement" whereby reading isn't simply living "in the moment" but rather living in the "re-examined moment."

Several individuals described their commonplace book as a reference to be used at a later date for a paper, book review, or letter they were planning to write. Some also spoke of their early ambition to become a writer and their hope that copying memorable sections from the books of authors they admired might aid them in learning the tools of the craft. Another wrote of the pleasure derived from sharing her passages with others: "They are all the more precious when I am inspired to impart them to others, to give them pleasure or solace, or to broaden their horizons of understanding when they ask this of me." And several expressed the belief that copying passages would in some mysterious way work its way into the mind so that it would heighten their appreciation of the world and expand their overall literary and personal sensibility. As one reader put it:

> I've had to trust that all reading goes into the unconscious where it builds a database, so to speak, that gives me intuitive purchase on assessing and understanding the world. Or that serves as a deeply rich palette from which I draw my own creative works, or apply my critical sense.

Because of its eloquence and insight and because it conveys so well the importance of the recording process itself, I would like to cite portions of one person's answer to the question why they keep a commonplace book.[21]

> I like the ritual of finding quotes that mean something to me (quotes that I find beautiful, truthful, challenging, etc.). I like typing them or writing them down (the actual physical act of doing this), and I like re-reading them once I've collected them. I like the deliberate search for quotes, as well as the surprise of stumbling upon them unexpectedly as I'm reading. It's

21 Olivia Dresher, writer, publisher of Impassio Press www.impassio.com and director of the Life Writing Connection, www.lifewriting.org.

like finding buried treasure and then rescuing it and finding a safe place for it. I rescue the words from the page of many (sometimes too many) words; otherwise, they would be lost. I find these gems and then collect them for safekeeping; my quote books have become treasure trunks.

When I write down a thought or expression—when I make it my own—it becomes more alive and valuable. To read a passage I love that I do not write down is like discarding or ignoring something of value... something that could be of future importance as a companion during hard times. Words are companions, lifeboats.

When I write something down, I make it mine by entering the thought or expression more fully. And, by writing it down, I make it "permanent" rather than fleeting. To write down a line or paragraph is a way to naturally pause and drink in the words. To isolate words as a quote (to remove them from the crowd of words) is a way of honoring them. I can't imagine reading a book without stopping to mark or quote passages at least a few times per reading. Quoting slows down my reading and connects me to the writer, whereas just reading (without pausing to quote) is the feeling of rushing and not stopping to touch the words in a more intimate way. And a quote is a world complete in itself....

Notes, fragments, quotes: these have become a way of

life for me, the way I approach life and the way I express. I imagine that not having a notebook to write in would be like a musician not having an instrument to play music on. I approach words as a way of being, or one key way of being. Words, music, films, art, nature—these are the pieces of my life.

Handwriting vs. Typing

In thinking further about the various answers individuals made on the survey, I also came to realize how critical the act of recording is to commonplacing. Reading the text is one thing. Recalling it is another. But in between these two activities is the process of transcribing. In copying the passages by pen or by typing, a reader is doing more than preserving them for future reference.

What is copying? First it is attending once again to the text. Perhaps it is also thinking about it further; it occupies your mind once again. David Michael Levin has compared transcribing to the hand copying of religious texts by medieval monks, an activity that required "the most intense meditative concentration, poise and steadiness of hand."[22] Later he spoke of it as a "way of carving words (and their meaning) into flesh, into body."

In a subsequent exchange about her survey responses, Olivia Dresher went further to suggest that transcribing the quotes by

22 David Michael Levin. *The Body's Recollection of Being: Phenomenological Psychology and the Deconstruction of Nihilism*, 1985. London: Routledge & Kegan Paul Books Ltd.

hand is superior to typing them on a typewriter which in turn is superior to typing them on a computer keyboard. She claimed: "handwritten quotes linger more in my consciousness because I actually wrote [sometimes very slowly] them with my hands into a notebook. And they feel more permanent (even if that's an illusion), more connected to me, less fleeting." For Levin and Dresher, writing the passages by hand is an experience that is almost "sacred," a feature of commonplacing that brings the meaning of the words into their consciousness in a far deeper way than when they are typed. The experience becomes a very physical one for them, one that is not unlike incorporating something into your body, as one does in eating food. As Borenstein noted in quoting the Talmud: "A fitting quotation is like bread to the famished."

Further Dresher went on to argue that while typing passages on a typewriter enables you to see them on a piece of paper, it doesn't have the same effects as writing them by hand. And that typing them on a computer keyboard, where they appear on the screen, places the text at an even further distance from the person than either of the two other methods of transcribing.

The distinction these readers make between the several methods of transcribing the passages in their commonplace book is instructive. So too are their claims for their short and long term effects on the transcriber. Does it matter how you record the passages? The hypothesis these readers propose is testable. It would be easy to design an experiment to compare the relative effects of the different methods of transcription. Consider a recall test or some other measure of permanence. Would quotes that had been handwritten be recalled with greater accuracy than those that had been typed on a typewriter or computer keyboard? That is but one of several questions that might be explored in such an experiment.

Earlier I suggested that the desire to preserve memorable reading passages must reflect a fundamental feature of the reading experience, leaving open the question of what that might be. The comments of those who responded to the survey question on this topic provide an answer. We keep a commonplace book to compensate for the fragility of our memory. Readers cannot hope to remember but a fraction of what they read. Memory is elusive, unreliable, plays tricks on us, and has a very limited capacity. A commonplace book is how a reader can surmount these limitations. Preserving passages of literary excellence permits us to revisit them at any time. We can review and reconsider those passages as often as we like; we can reengage ourselves with the text and experience once again its truths. No one likes to forget moments of aesthetic beauty or insight. A camera preserves them as visual images. A commonplace book preserves them as words.

The Electronic Future

I have this habit of turning down corners of pages that contain something I like. Sometimes I'll write in a book, but I try to avoid it. It's so messy.
Sara Nelson, *So Many Books So Little Time*

When Ben Jonson was a small boy, his tutor, William Camden, persuaded him of the virtue of keeping a commonplace book: pages where an ardent reader might copy down passages that especially pleased him, preserving sentences that seemed particularly apt or wise or rightly formed, and which would, because they were written afresh in a new place, and in a context of favor, be better remembered, as if they were being set down at the same time in the memory of the mind.
William H. Gass, *A Temple of Texts*

From the earliest days of the commonplace book tradition, copying noteworthy passages by hand, usually into one or more notebooks, has been the preferred method of transcription. The introduction of the typewriter and more recently the computer has made inroads on this practice, although only one of the individuals who responded to the survey said he was now keeping his commonplace book in electronic form.

Nevertheless, in recent years a considerable number of commonplace books and quotation lists have appeared on the Web. While these electronic analogues of their printed forerunners have probably not led to a revival of the commonplace tradition, it has surely broadened the audience for what had become a largely private activity.

At the same time it has raised anew in my mind the question of how to define a commonplace book. Is it a patchwork collection of quotations or must the quotes be organized in some fashion to qualify as a commonplace book? In the Preface to her scholarly treatment of Renaissance commonplace books, Ann Moss writes:

> *The subject of my research, the commonplace book, in the form which was normative to it by the end of the sixteenth century, was a collection of quotations (usually Latin quotations) culled from authors held to be authoritative, or at any rate, commendable in their opinions, and regarded as exemplary in terms of linguistic usage and stylistic niceties. The feature which distinguished the commonplace book from any random collection of quotations was the fact that the selected extracts were gathered together under heads.*[23]

If the extracts must be organized around heads or general topics, most of the commonplace websites would have to be considered so in name only. This is also true for the majority of

23 Ann Moss. *Printed Commonplace-Books and the Structuring of Renaissance Thought*, 1966. New York: Oxford University Press.

privately maintained commonplace books that, by and large, are neither organized topically nor annotated to any extent. At the same time I think it is important to appreciate the evolving nature of the commonplace tradition. In antiquity and the Renaissance commonplace books were viewed as a source of the knowledge and wisdom of the time. Now that we have other vastly more powerful means of organizing knowledge, it is clear that it is no longer necessary to treat them in quite such a restricted fashion.

To be sure, collecting notable thoughts remains a powerful desire for many readers. The legacy of early commonplace books provides a model. Websites that label their collection as a Commonplace Book maintain the tradition of this time honored practice. I tend to view a modern commonplace book, then, as a collection of quotations that an individual, during the course of their reading experience, has found notable or significant in some respect. This would exclude a large book of quotations that has been selected by a staff of people for commercial purposes, such as *Bartlett's Book of Quotations*.

Thus, it now seems to me that the act of transcribing memorable literary passages, either by hand, typing, or at a computer keyboard is the *sin qua non* of a genuine commonplace book. There are two groups of sites on the web that can be characterized this way. While the boundaries between the two are not precise, the first are labeled Commonplace Books, while the second are Quotation Collections or Archives. A representative selection of each group are listed in Tables 3 and 4, respectively.

Table 3
Representative Commonplace Book Websites

Reading and Writing the Commonplace—A Hypertext Model
http://www.cmu.ca/faculty/pdyck/old/cpbface.htm

J. Jacobs A Commonplace Book http://3stages.org/quotes

The Constant Reader's Commonplace Book
http://www.constantreader.org/v2/commonplace.html

Identity Theory Commonplace Book
http://www.identitytheory.com/etexts/commonplace.html

Scott McLemee's Commonplace Book
http://www.mclemee.com/id8.html

M. Kuchling's Commonplace Book
http://www.amk.ca/quotations/quotations

Verbatim Commonplace Book http://shanta.edublogs.org

Risa's Commonplace Book http://epud.net/~bears/common.html

The Advisor's Commonplace Book
http://www.psu.edu/dus/leonard/book

The Sheila Variations
http://www.sheilaomalley.com/archives/cat_commonplace.html

Several of these sites include a section in which the author gives a brief statement of their background. For example the author of The Sheila Variations, http://www.sheilaomalley.com/archives/cat_commonplace.html, writes:

Years ago-in high school-I started keeping a "commonplace book" - although I had no idea at the time that there was a NAME for it. I just wanted to keep all the quotes I really liked in one place. I called it my quote book. Then much later, I realized that there's a long, long tradition of people keeping these "commonplace books"-especially "those guys" that I love so much in the 18th century. I've shared a ton of those quotes with you all here.

The author of the Quotations Archive, http://www.aphids.com/ quotes/index.shtml, writes:

I started this collection of quotations in mid-1993 when I started a job administering a unix machine in a university computer lab. I was looking for a way to motivate people to read the login message (where we often try to communicate problems or new features to users). I decided a new quotation every weekday might make people pay attention to the messages.

The Hypertext site at http://www.cmu.ca/faculty/pdyck/ old/cpbface.htm is perhaps the most unusual of those shown in either table. Its author views the site as an experimental electronic essay on commonplace books organized in hypertext. In a sense the site is an annotated commonplace book on the subject of commonplace books. Since the material is formatted in hypertext, it can be read in whatever order the reader chooses, rather than sequentially as in an ordinary printed document or other pages on the web. The site is largely a historical and analytical presentation of the commonplace book concept interspersed with electronic links to illustrative examples.

For example, under the heading Reading/Writing the Commonplaces, there is the following Primary Material link to a passage by Erasmus titled *On what to take note of*:

> *Erasmus, in his* De ratione studii ac legendi interpretandique autores liber, *trains his reader to: take careful note in your reading of striking words; archaic or novel expressions; cleverly devised or neatly turned arguments; and any outstanding elegance of style, any adages, historical parallels, and general statements that are worth remembering. These passages should be indicated by some appropriate mark. (Quoted in Mohl, 410)*

Following this passage there is a link back to the section Reading/Writing the Commonplaces. Sometimes additional links are embedded within the quoted passages that, in turn, take the reader on another path through the material. At the bottom of every page, however, there is always a link back to the original index ("layout") so that the reader can proceed in a relatively straightforward way through the material or to whatever topic he or she chooses.

Another unusual Commonplace Book website is authored by a librarian, J. Jacobs, at http://3stages.org/quotes/. It is distinctive in that it has an author and word index, as well as a search tool for specific topics and "random quotes." To locate the passages that Jacobs has entered into his Commonplace Book, it is first necessary to type the name of a topic, word, or author in the box on the search page. An author search for Shakespeare resulted in three selections, one for Borges yielded eleven, and a topic search for "Literature" yielded over a dozen passages, some of considerable length. For example, the search for Hemingway produced the following passages that seem most timely at the time of this writing:

> *No one man nor group of men incapable of fighting or exempt from fighting should in any way be given the power, no matter how gradually it is given them, to put this country or any country into war.*

> *The first panacea for a mismanaged nation is inflation of the currency; the second is war. Both bring a temporary prosperity; both bring a permanent ruin. But both are the refuge of political and economic opportunists.*
> Ernest Hemingway from "Notes on the Next War" *in American Points of View.* 1936

Although the indexing feature of this site readily facilitates a secondary ordering of specific topics, none of the collector's quotations were annotated. Instead they were selected because they were found to be "particularly beautiful or insightful or funny or just plain memorable." The author also notes that they were recorded "for myself so that I can get back to them easily since, for me, 'memorable' does not always translate into I have memorized it," another advantage to his indexing tools.

Two of the electronic commonplace books shown in Table 3 are designed as collective sites, a Wiki in Internet parlance, where anyone can contribute to the list of passages. The Literary Work Commonplace Book on one of the Wikiquote pages, http://en.wikiquote.org/wiki/List_of_literary_works consists of an unedited collection of quotations drawn from a list of book titles arranged alphabetically. For example, a click on the link for *The American Scene* by Henry James displays 17 passages including their page and chapter number, while the link for Charles Dickens' *A Tale of Two Cities* cites 19 passages with their chapter number. The Wikiquote section of literary works includes similar selections for hundreds of well-known books.

The Commonplace Book for Advisors, http://www.psu.edu/dus/leonard/book is a useful collection of quotations that educators might find instructive in guiding and supporting their students. It has been created by the voluntary submissions of unknown advisors from unknown places. Most importantly, it is organized around a set of fourteen topics including careers, decision making, overcoming adversity, success and friendship.

With one exception, the remaining websites listed in Table 3 consist of a cumulative set of quotations and sometimes drawings and photographs from literary or artistic sources on various topics that bear no relationship with one another other than they follow one another in chronological order. The exception is *Risa's Commonplace Book* at http://epud.net/~bears/common.html, in so far as it clearly focuses on "ideas about perception, language, and art." The sometimes rather complex, as well as lengthy passages on this website are listed alphabetically by author's last name and, like the Hyptertext Model, http://www.cmu.ca/faculty/pdyck/old/cpblayot.htm, is distinctive in that the author has contributed notes or comments, sometimes rather lengthy, in response to the majority of her citations. For example, she quotes and then comments on William James as follows:

James, William. *The Principles of Psychology.* London: Macmillan, 1901. [BF121.J2]
Every definite image in the mind is steeped and dyed in the free water that flows round it. With it goes the sense of its relations, near and remote, the dying echo of whence it came to us, the dawning sense of whither it is to lead. The significance, the value, of the image is all in this halo or penumbra that surrounds and escorts it . . . (255).

It is amazing how much of what one reads in Kimble (1988) on psychobiology is already found in James (1901). But this passage, although implicit in Kimble, is explicit in James: context makes the image. It might not be too much to say, exceeding James: image is the information (text) that we find when we examine the field (con-text). That is, the text does not merely depend on the context, but is a consequence of our examination of context, which is actually all that is there. See also Peirce.

I was greatly impressed by Risa's Commonplace Book website. Perhaps because it dealt with subjects (philosophy and psychology) that have preoccupied much of my academic work, I found myself spending a good deal of time reading the material on her website. With the addition of her comments, it also illustrated the very best of the commonplace book tradition—provocative passages combined with thoughtful annotations.

The Quotation Websites shown in Table 4 consist of a wide-ranging selection of maxims, proverbs and aphorisms, as well as short, pity statements on a host of topics. All of them are also organized by heads or subjects. For example the Quote Garden, http://www.quotegarden.com, lists hundreds of subject links each taking the reader to a new web page with a series of quotations on that topic. The first, Abortion, lists fifteen different quotes, while the last, Yoga, lists twenty-four, followed by an additional set of links to Hatha, Pranayama Yoga, Yoga Postures, and Kriya Yoga.

Some of the sites also focus on more specific issues or individuals. The site maintained by Dr. Gabriel Robbins, a computer science professor, http://www.cs.virginia.edu/~robins/quotes.html, is devoted to remarks of "famous people." While not organized in any systematic fashion, they are uniformly short, sometimes sly and sometimes humorous remarks that often give one pause. For instance,

> *"Glory is fleeting, but obscurity is forever."*
> Napoleon Bonaparte

Table 4
Representative Quotation Websites

Quote Garden http://www.quotegarden.com

Quotations Archive http://www.aphids.com/quotes/index.shtml

Quotations http://www.theotherpages.org/quote.html

The Quotations Page http://www.quotationspage.com

Generation Terrorists
http://www.generationterrorists.com/index_quotes.shtml

Quoteland http://www.quoteland.com

Dr. Gabriel Robbins Quotes
http://www.cs.virginia.edu/~robins/quotes.html

Quote Geek http://www.quotegeek.com

Library Quotations http://www.ifla.org/I/humour/subj.htm

Wisdom Quotes http://www.wisdomquotes.com

Lit Quotes http://www.litquotes.com

"Victory goes to the player who makes the next-to-last mistake."
Chessmaster Savielly Grigorievitch Tartakower

"His ignorance is encyclopedic"
Abba Eban

"Give me chastity and continence, but not yet."
Saint Augustine

"A lie gets halfway around the world before the truth has a chance to get its pants on."
Sir Winston Churchill (1874-1965)

The Literature Quotation site, http://www.litquotes.com is arranged by author, book title, and an unusual section labeled Lit Quotes Duo where a new pair of quotations is presented each day that "may be similar, surprising or contradictory. They can make you smile or make you think." The Duo for the day I am writing is:

"I remember a mass of things, but nothing distinctly; a quarrel, but nothing wherefore. O God, that men should put an enemy in their mouths to steal away their brains!"
Shakespeare, *Othello*

"I see that a man cannot give himself up to drinking without being miserable one-half his days and mad the other... "
Anne Bronte, *The Tenant of Wildfell Hall*

Finally, the author of the Wisdom Quotes, http://www.wisdomquotes.com introduces the site with a statement that is thoroughly consistent with the commonplace book tradition:

Welcome to the Wisdom Quotes site! I've put some of

my favorite quotes here, and I try to update with new
quotations often. I try to be selective in picking quotes,
including only those quotes that I find challenging or
inspiring or interesting—in other words, reflecting my
own tastes and philosophy.

She has also organized her site around almost 300 separate subject links ranging from Action to Writing and invites readers to subscribe to a Wisdom Quotes e-mail list, promising to send subscribers one of her selections from time to time.

At the outset of this project I assumed that collecting quotes in a commonplace book was an uncommon and fairly private activity. Early on I discovered that only a few commonplace books have been published, largely the works of reasonably well-known authors, and none have been widely read. But I had no idea that so many had entered the public domain in the form of websites. There are currently countless quotation sites on the Web and a somewhat lesser number that refer to themselves as commonplace books.

In a few exchanges with the authors of these sites, I inquired why they had gone to the effort of posting their selections on the Web, rather than keeping them in a private document. One individual responded: "Why not? Publishing things to the Web costs me nothing, so my general policy is to publish any data or documents that I spend time assembling." Another said her website was "a way for friends and visitors to share quotes that they love. I liked the idea of the exchange of authors among reading friends. In a private journal we wouldn't really be sharing them! As a librarian, my inclination is to share information and ideas."

The lure of the Internet is undeniable. It makes creating a website, and now a blog, almost as easy as writing a letter or sending an e-mail. In addition, the software, especially for blogs, greatly facilitates the organization of the material in any conceptual or topical arrangement the author wishes. But does its public visibility also increase its readership?

In response to my question about the number of hits or visits their websites get during an average week, one author said about fifty to seventy-five hits a week, another said 150 each week, while the author of the most widely visited said his gets about 762 during an average week. On a yearly basis, this ranges from about 2,600 to 39,624, an enormous degree of variability that surely depends on the subject matter of the website, as well as its placement in Internet search engines. Regardless, it is clear that readership on the Web is far greater than what would be expected for a printed volume of the same material. Of course, these figures tell us nothing about how much is read or what a viewer derives from the experience.

A Closer Look

Then I was seized with an idea: I would copy out my favourite passages from Ursule Mirouet, word for word....It was the first time in my life that I had felt any desire to copy sentences from a book. I ransacked the room for paper, but all I could find was a few sheets of notepaper intended for letters to our parents....I decided I would write directly onto the inside of my sheepskin coat.

Dai Sijie, *Balzac & the Little Chinese Seamstress*

In your luckiest moments of reading, it seems to me, what you find is something to keep quiet about. You find something to hoard. You come upon one of those inexplicable places in a book that touches you so deeply you don't even have the words to say why. And you should not have to. These places belong to you. Others can just go find their own.

Suzanne Freeman, *American Scholar Winter 2005*

My original goal in beginning this project was to look more closely at the entries in my Commonplace Book in order to determine what they might reveal about the central concerns of my life. It was planned in the manner of any self-analysis. The passages were never selected with the expectation that I or anyone else would one day embark on this task. As a result they convey a relatively "unbiased" view of the beliefs and feelings that seemed significant to me at the time they were chosen.[24] I thought that by looking at them closely, I might obtain a deeper understanding of myself and the issues that I have been preoccupied with over the course of my reading life.

I realize that this presentation may be of little interest to anyone but myself or that the data that I present have any degree of generality. While it may have the appearance of social science research, it is, in fact, a case study in which I have applied a simple method of measurement in an informal study of my own Commonplace Book. Perhaps this presentation will suggest an approach that other individuals who keep a commonplace book might find useful. It is within this framework that I invite readers to view the results of my own analysis.

At the outset I thought it would be interesting to make note of the type of material that I drew upon in creating my Commonplace Book. Table 5 compares the number of Fiction and Non-Fiction works that I read over the years that I have been collecting passages. Of the total (N = 242) separate works I read, fiction dominates the selections with approximately two-thirds (N = 145) drawn from this genre, with the majority

25 In the language of social researchers they constituted a non-reactive measure, one taken when individuals are not aware they are being studied. Under these conditions, it is assumed that they behave the way they truly feel since they are not trying to please the experimenter, confirm his hypothesis, or behave in a normative fashion.

Table 5

Analysis of Reading Material

Non-Fiction	
Periodical*	61
Non-Fiction Book	36
Fiction	
Short Story	24
Verse	16
Fiction Book	102
Drama	2
Total Fiction	145
Total Non-Fiction	97
Total	242

Note: "Periodical" refers to any non-fiction essay, interview, reflection, memoir, or profile.

represented by contemporary rather than classical novels (N = 102). The remaining selections were drawn from non-fiction sources (N = 97) with almost two-thirds of these from literary periodicals (N = 61).

Rather than wade through every one of the almost three hundred pages of my Commonplace Book, I decided to simplify the task somewhat by classifying a representative sample of passages. I began with the first block of thirty-five pages. Then I skipped the following thirty pages, then classified those on the next thirty-five pages, skipped the next thirty, and so on until the end. This yielded five separate blocks of thirty-five pages in each of which I attempted to classify the selections I had copied over the past twenty years.

It was not always easy to decide how to classify a passage. This was especially true for the Briefs, but sometimes also for the longer passages, and the Quotes. Some were rather enigmatic and I could not reconstruct why I had made note of them in the first place, as in: *Whole lot of heavy thinking going on out there*. Others were brief phrases or collections of colorful words without any general meaning that I could detect, such as *Manny's car wash blues...* Still others were simply unclassifiable because they were vague or difficult to interpret: *It's like a swamp—there are these mangrove trees growing out of it that are quite amazing*.

I often copy a passage because it is clever or humorous but on review, I could not find any conceptual basis to classify them in this study, such as this passage from an essay by Anthony Lane in the *New Yorker*:

> *Is there some law that prevents Tom Hanks from winning the Oscar for the Best Actor forever? The answer is yes. There is such a law. It is the law of the three-year limit, otherwise known as the Iron Law of Stardom ....There is no penalty for breaking this law, for the simple reason that it is unbreakable....This is the true a priori, the reality that explains all other realities.*

Similarly a number of passages were written so beautifully and so artfully that they almost commanded a mark in the margin but did not readily lend themselves to classification.

> *In the late summer of that year we lived in a house in a village that looked across the river and the plain to the mountains. In the bed of the river there were pebbles and boulders, dry and white in the sun, and the water was clear and swiftly moving and blue in the channels. Troops went by the house and down the road and the dust they raised powdered the leaves of the trees. The trunks of the trees too were dusty and the leaves fell early that year…*[25]

But by and large most of the passages, especially the longer ones, conveyed a clear and coherent idea that fell into one of the themes that emerged as I went along from page to page.

To get a sense of my scheme, I will briefly define each of the twelve most frequently occurring categories and present an example, along with its source. These categories were selected because they met an arbitrary criterion of at least thirty citations out of the 1,115 that I recorded. Each of the illustrative examples has been taken from what was, at the time I undertook the analysis in June of 2005, the last set of passages.

Literature: Citations that treat poetry, fiction, and non-fiction as well as descriptions of the reading experience, specific authors, and the relationship between literature and life.

---

25 Ernest Hemingway *A Farewell to Arms*, 1929. New York: Charles Scribner's Sons.

A novel like poetry, can be more or less insightful, more or less profound. It can certainly be more or less moving. It can even be moral or immoral. But, being fiction, it cannot be true or false in the way that an empirical proposition is true or false.
Elliot Perlman, *Seven Types of Ambiguity*

Romance: Expressions of love, romantic feelings, and devotion to another person, including a spouse, lover or muse.

In the ten years since the car crash took her from him, he had cherished her more than while she was alive. Julius sometimes heaved with despair when he thought of how his lush contentment with Miriam, the true idyllic soaring moments of life, had come and gone without his fully grasping them....He knew also that no other woman would ever really matter to him.
Irving Yalom, *The Schopenhauer Cure*

Learning: The pleasure and importance of scholarly life and one devoted to research, critical reflection, and analysis.

...just don't imagine life as a complete learned man to be too delightful...It is a tiring, troublesome life full of work; only the delight in doing it gives it its charm. One doesn't get rich with it...
Irving Yalom, *The Schopenhauer Cure*

Change: Statements that describe the factors that are most likely to lead to a change in a person's beliefs and behaviors and the results of various influence techniques.

The people who can make a bold move at a given moment are those who are not constrained economically, culturally or socially. That's why those who grew up in the elite and have the power to impact things have a responsibility to change the face of society.
Ronit Chacham, *Breaking Ranks*

Writing*:* Characterizations of the writing life, its difficulties and importance, including references to particular writing routines and how one learns to write more effectively.

It [Graham Greene's *The Heart of the Matter*] made a strong impression: that one could write with such apparent simplicity of the daily complications and pain of a usual existence, a baffled sensibility.
Shirley Hazzard, *Paris Review* #173

Age*:* The effects of growing older, how others perceive and treat the aged, and how one confronts the increasing problems of old age.

She's probably no older than me. In fact, she's my future—the wart, the walker, the wheelchair. As she came closer, he heard her mumbling.
Irving Yalom, *The Schopenhauer Cure*

Self: How we come to know ourselves, the effect we have on others, and the nature of personal identity, as well as differences between the private and public self.

She moved in a manner that suggested she was completely comfortable in her skin.
Elliot Perlman, *Seven Types of Ambiguity*

Relationships: a description of the way in which two or more people are linked to one another or an expression about how one feels about the nature of relationships with other people.

In our friendship we were able to share our private thoughts and ideas, to test them upon one another, in a way that would have been impossible had we been linked more closely by ties which, paradoxically enough, separate more profoundly than they join, though human illusion forbids us to believe this.
Lawrence Durrell, *Justine*

Marriage: Descriptions of the marital experience, including its joys and limitations, and the course of a marital relationship over time.

What a feat of social engineering to shoehorn an entire citizenry (minus the occasional straggler) into such uniform household arrangements, all because everyone knows that true love demands it and that any reluctance to participate signals an insufficiency of love.
Laura Kipnis, *Against Love: A Polemic*

Alienation: Expressions of isolation, despair, depression and a general sense of melancholy, including death and dying.

> *I was just not cut out for the business of living at a time like this, a time when wondering, caring, dreaming...they were just not selling, they were uncool, unhip, not sexy, past their expiration date...Some other time maybe.*
> Elliot Perlman, *Seven Types of Ambiguity*

Understanding: Statements about explanation in general, the search for truth, and how to most effectively arrive at some degree of knowledge or insight about a person or event

> *...statistical probabilities aren't the same as truths.*
> Ian McEwan, *Saturday*

Solitude: The emotional and intellectual experience of being alone, its effects and values, as well as particular examples of a solitary life and why individuals seek it.

> *...the less I have to do with people, the happier I am. When I tried living in life, I was drawn into agitation. To stay out of life, to want nothing and to expect nothing, to keep myself engaged in elevated contemplative pursuits—that is the path, my only path, to peace.*
> Elliot Perlman, *Seven Types of Ambiguity*

After I had completed classifying the passages, I indexed each block of thirty-five pages by category using the page number in the Commonplace Book where it appeared. This provided a tally of the frequency of each category for that block and then, after combining the data for each block, an overall picture of my record keeping-activity.

The pyramid in Table 6 displays the sixty different categories that emerged in this analysis in terms of the frequency of their occurrence. Some of the categories were rarely noted. For example, I recorded only one expression of Hope, and three of

Table 6

Indicates the approximate frequency of each category, as shown in the boxes on the left edge for each category in the center section of the pyramid, with those at the apex the most frequent and those at the base the least.

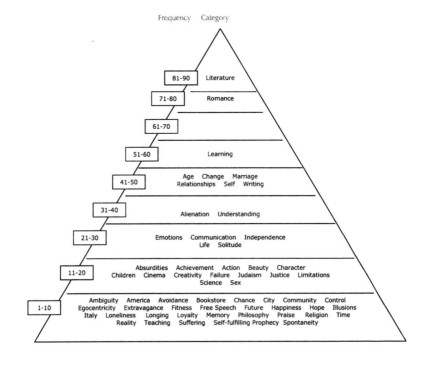

Ambiguity, Happiness, Philosophy and the Self-Fulfilling Prophecy. I noted the concept Loyalty nine times, although it appeared in only one document.[26] Additional categories with at least fifteen citations included Action (as distinguished from belief), Beauty, Character, Children, Communication, Emotions, Failure, Morality, and Life (ordinary daily activities and/or struggles).

Taken together the most frequently cited categories represented slightly more than 50% of all the recorded classifications in this analysis. This leaves open the question of whether this was the result of a certain uniformity in my classifying procedure or the nature of the reading material itself which was no doubt chosen, in part, because it dealt with those topics.

In general there was considerable consistency in the highest-ranking categories for each block of recorded pages. Both Literature and Romance were among the most frequent in each of the five blocks, while Change, Learning and Age appeared in all but one. Two others, Marriage and Self, were in the most frequent list in all but two of the five blocks. I had anticipated that the themes might vary both in their content and frequency over time so that those I was most likely to choose in the beginning would not be the same twenty years later. But this was not the case, as the category frequencies remained relatively constant throughout this period. And on reflection this doesn't surprise me after all. I am still the same bookish student and incurable romantic that I have always been, and was even long before I began transcribing passages from the books that I read.

26 Henry Louis Gates, Jr., The End of Loyalty, *The New Yorker*, March 9, 1998.

In Table 7, I have summarized the frequency of the most-cited categories in my analysis. It shows, for example, that Solitude was noted thirty times, while each of the remaining categories appeared increasingly more often with Literature reaching a value of eighty-seven, almost three times more frequent than Solitude. As documented in Table 7, each of these categories still appeared considerably more often than the majority of the thirty others.

Table 7

Displays the total frequency of each of the twelve most frequency cited categories.

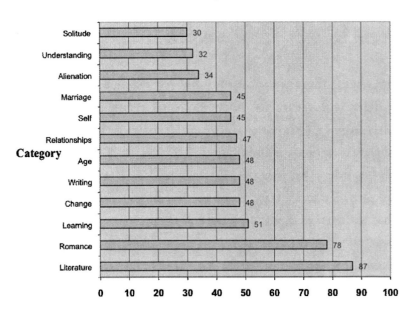

Patterns Among the Passages

For some time since her operation, and without publication its goal, she had been jotting down without order or pattern, anecdotes gleaned from the late nineteenth and twentieth centuries, noting down those matters or events which moved her. One day these notes and fragments of thought might form a coherent mosaic and reveal to her her own spiritual autobiography as well as biography of her time.
Frederic Tuten, *The Green House*

I had a friend attempt to categorize my books once and she said she had a much deeper appreciation for me as a person when she was done.
William Boyd, *Brazzaville Beach*

Independently of my own reading proclivities, the Commonplace Book that I have kept for many years stands alone as a collection of noteworthy ideas, some thoughtful, some provocative, some a little odd, or clever or novel in some way. The significance of the passages that I have copied does not depend on the fact that I selected them. Rather they are the words of writers of serious literature, both fiction and non-fiction, that might give anyone pause for thought. I secretly harbor the wish that my collection might one day be read by readers who share an interest in this sort of material or perhaps a student who is investigating contemporary commonplace books might find something of value in it.[27]

In one sense my Commonplace Book has become something of a substitute for a personal journal, a document that long ago I abandoned. For instance, not a day goes by now that I don't think of the experience of growing old and what it is doing to me. And were I in the habit of keeping a journal I would no doubt write far too much about it. Instead, every once in a while I read something about aging that strikes me as especially relevant to my life and so it becomes a passage in my Commonplace Book, subsequently to be classified under the category of Aging. The same is true for almost all of the categories that appear most frequently in my collection.

It is also true that my Commonplace Book is an account of the increasing importance of literature in my life. Why did I even bother to begin this record and now why do I continue? It is no more than appreciating the thoughts, ideas, and questions that I encounter on the pages of the literature I read. I want to preserve them, revisit them, and reconsider them now and again. The experience is not unlike one of viewing any attractive object. I want to take another look or look a little longer. So I mark the passage and eventually add it to my Commonplace Book so that I can reread it again and think further about it as often as I like.

27 In his *New York Times* article on commonplace books, Cole notes that: "There is no extensive literature on the commonplace book. I have a friend who [reports that] she could find nothing about commonplace books from her colleagues nor from any of the usual lit histories."

To be sure, the passages were selected and thereby valued because of my idiosyncratic personality and background. I wanted to save them, gather them in, squirrel them away. Others feel that way about antiques or fine cars or wine or works of art. I feel that way about ideas. I collect them like others collect rare books. Indeed, the ideas are often rare and for that reason take on additional value. The process has become as much a part of my life as eating and sleeping. No doubt other readers of the same materials would squirrel away a different set of passages. And some of them may be attracted to the passages that I have marked for reasons that have little to do with mine. Perhaps a comparative study of the passages marked by readers of the same book might shed light on this very interesting process.

As I have gone through the passages, I have begun to get a handle on why I was drawn to them in the first place. While some are simply amusing or witty expressions or written so well I simply had to make note of them, the majority convey an important truth, a truth that I have found in literature or a proposed truth that calls for inquiry. Like other readers, I am drawn to literature for many reasons but among the foremost are the truths that I find there. I never know when they will be found or what writers and in which of their books, I will chance upon these truths. Their discovery is unpredictable, unexpected, surprising. The experience is one of the most powerful effects of reading literature. On review, I've concluded that the majority of these truths are propositions that fall into one of four categories, each of which is defined below, followed by an example.

Belief Confirmation: A passage that reinforces a belief or value that I hold, often one that is not widely held, or one that becomes clearer when seen on the page.

Ian McEwan's *Saturday* contains a great many passages of this kind. I marked forty-five separate passages in this intellectually rich novel about a single day in the life of Henry Perowne, a British neurosurgeon. Throughout this tale Perowne muses about his discipline, his family, the routine chores that occupy his day, and the troublesome times in which he lives during the early years of the 21st century. In turn, I was led to reflect on those same topics as I paused to place my marks in the margin and then to ponder his musings and the extent to which I agreed with them or not. As a result, although it was not a very lengthy novel, it took me forever to read—a pleasure devoutly treasured by this reader.

Throughout, McEwan speculates about the origins of human behavior and difficulties of identifying them with any precision. Since I have been concerned with those very same issues throughout my professional life, I marked a goodly number where McEwan writes about this issue.

> *It's a commonplace of parenting and modern genetics that parents have little or no influence on the characters of their children. You never know who you are going to get. Opportunities, health, prospects, accent, table manners—these might lie within your power to shape. But what really determines the sort of person who's coming to live with you is which sperm finds which egg, how the cards in the two packs*

are chosen, then how they are shuffled, halved and spliced at the moment of recombination. Cheerful or neurotic, kind or greedy, curious or dull, expansive or shy and anywhere in between; it can be quite an affront to parental self-regard, just how much of the work has already been done.

Who could ever reckon up the damage done to love and friendship and all hopes of happiness by a surfeit or depletion of this or that neurotransmitter?

But can anyone really know the sign, the tell of an honest man? There's been some good work on this very question. Perowne has read Paul Ekman on the subject. In the smile of a self-conscious liar certain muscle groups in the face are not activated. They only come to life as the expression of genuine feeling. The smile of a deceiver is flawed, insufficient.

Personal Confirmation: A passage that reveals something about myself (or one that I had not recognized before), as well as a correspondence between some aspect of my life and a character in a story, most likely one that I identify with in some respect.

For example, in this analysis I recorded twelve separate descriptions of what I call the two-selves experience. I classified them in the group labeled Self and taken together they constituted a little over a quarter (27 per cent) of the forty-five Self-related passages. My favorite is drawn from a famous Chekhov short story:

He had two lives; one obvious, which every one could see and know, if they were sufficiently interested, a life full of conventional truth and conventional fraud, exactly like the lives of his friends and acquaintances; and another, which moved underground. And by a strange conspiracy of circumstances, everything that was to him important, interesting, vital, everything than enabled him to be sincere and denied self-deception and was the very core of his being, must dwell hidden away from others, and everything that made him false, a mere shape in which he hid himself in order to conceal the truth, as for instance his work in the bank, arguments at the club, his favorite gibe about women, going to parties with his wife—all this was open.

Anton Chekhov, *The Lady with the Toy Dog*

Others have also described the experience well:

Always while one part of him spoke, another part stood on one side and wondered, "Is this who I am speaking? Can I really exist like this?

Graham Greene, *The Man Within*

Everyone he knew carried with them the aura of another life which was half-secret and half-open, to be known about but not mentioned...He remembered the shock when he first came to know Paris, the culture of easy duplicity, the sense he got of these men and women, watched over by the novelists, casually

withholding what mattered to them most.
Colm Toibin, *The Master*

These passages were also marked because they correspond to an enduring duality in my life, between my work as a social scientist and as a newly arrived student of literature. Trying to embrace these often-contradictory forces has been a continuing challenge, one that I do not shun, but rather find quite worth exploring. I ask myself: Are these two cultures really incompatible? Cannot one hold simultaneously to the different forms of truth, to the general truths of science and the specific truths of literature?

In writing to me about this topic Audrey Borenstein quotes the following passage from her book *Redeeming the Sin: Social Science and Literature*:

The social scientist, too, needs experience, observation, and imagination; and the best of social science, the works that will endure, are those in which all three are interwoven. Yet, while the risk for the social scientist is that he may miss seeing the detail— the trees, the risk of the writer is that he may miss seeing the forest. It would seem that the social scientist and the writer work from different directions toward the same achievement, the discovery of the universal. Ultimately, however, the distinction between artistic and scientific endeavor is arbitrary and spurious...The crystal and the molecule, the spinning earth, the leaf moving in the wind are rightful subjects for both poet

and naturalist: artist and scientist are not two beings,
but one.

I have also come to believe that it isn't necessary to choose between these two cultures, that they go hand in hand, much like so many other so-called dualities that are said to characterize contemporary life, say for example between solitude and socializing, between marriage and autonomy, between the public and the private self. Clearly the issue has entered my Commonplace Book in a very salient fashion.

Hypothesis/Question: The passages in this group pose a question or put forward a hypothesis that seems original or usual in some respect, one that warrants inquiry or confirms a finding that I have read about before.

I often make note of such passages because they seem on occasion to be both surprising and illuminating. We don't normally think of literature as a source of hypotheses. Indeed, I know of no social scientist that carries out empirical research on literary issues or draws upon literary insights in any systematic fashion. The various social science disciplines might be enriched if they did. I have taken a few easily testable hypotheses drawn randomly from some of the works of fiction that I've recently read that illustrate this third class of passages from my Commonplace Book

> *Let's say there is only one thing we know about men:*
> *that they feel a tension between monogamy and*
> *promiscuity. Let's further say that the balance of that*

tension is different in different men, and that possibly the balance is inherited, and it changes as the men age, sometimes from monogamy toward promiscuity and sometimes from promiscuity toward monogamy.
Jane Smiley, *Why Marriage?*

As civilization advances, poetry declines.
Debra Weinstein, *Apprentice to the Flower Poet*

There is nothing worse than having been truly happy once in your life. From that moment on, everything makes you sad, even the most insignificant things.
Maxence Fermine, *The Black Violin*

Envy and cruelty inevitably accompany fame, however small that fame may be.
Siri Hustvedt, *What I Loved*

…the last thing we ever learn about ourselves is our effect.
William Boyd, *Brazzaville Beach*

Their inability to dance well is a sign of their inability to adapt themselves to the needs of their partners.
Azar Nafisi, *Reading Lolita in Tehran*

…essentially you could not persuade anyone to give up something that gave him intense pleasure.
Joseph Epstein, *Fabulous Small Jews*

In each instance, an intriguing proposition is proposed, one that

that lends itself to empirical inquiry. Several of these notions are non-obvious, some are provocative, while others may seem patently false. Still they are sufficiently in doubt in my mind, as well as sufficiently interesting, to warrant study. To be sure they appear in the books I read in a fairly unsystematic fashion, almost totally out of the blue it would seem. And because they originate in literature rather than science, they do not enter the research mainstream. The only place they make an appearance are in the books I read and then in my Commonplace Book, where they reside until perhaps one day they will be investigated empirically.

Noteworthy: There are, of course, other types of passages that have captured my attention or moved me deeply, but either by virtue of their mystery or distinctiveness do no fall into one of three other groups. Nevertheless, they are among the most important encounters that I've had as a reader.

> *That winter, when it was all over, I would walk or ride a bus past her building. Sometimes I'd think how lucky I'd been to have spent a year with her there and how gladly I would give everything I now had to be back with the same woman, staring out those windows whenever she went sulking into the other room, imagining and envying those strolling outside, never once suspecting that one day soon I might be a stroller, too, looking in envying the man I'd been there once, knowing all along, though that if I had to do it over again, I'd still end where I was, yearning for those days when I was living with a woman I had never loved and*

*would never love but in whose home I had...invented
a woman who, like me was neither here nor there.*
Andre Aciman, *Pensione Eolo in False Papers*

Summing Up

The truths conveyed by these passages may also be uniquely true
for me. That is the wonderful thing about literature: it makes no
claims of universality, it is not true or false in the way an empirical
proposition is. Rather we read ourselves *into* literature without
concern, as we are in science, for whether or not the passage is
true for others, and if so, for how many and to what degree.
Instead, the truth of any given passage is immediately true to the
reader because it corresponds to his or her experience or provides
a language for it in a way that had not been available before. "Yes,"
we say, "that is true for me. This is my story. That's exactly the
way I felt. I had not realized its truth until I saw it on the page."

Phyllis Rose expresses a similar view in her recent book on
Marcel Proust.[28]

> *...but what I looked forward to most in reading Proust
> were revelations about myself...Proust understood
> that every reader, in reading, reads himself. Far from
> minding this, he saw it as the writer's task to facilitate
> it. Thus the writer's word is merely a kind of optical
> instrument which he offers to the reader to enable him
> to discern what, without this book he would perhaps
> never have perceived in himself. And the recognition*

28 Phyllis Rose *The Year of Reading Proust* 2000. Washington, D.C.: Counter-
point Press.

by the reader in his own self of what the book says is proof of its veracity.

Here Rose suggests that the power of literature lies in confirming those truths about ourselves that we rarely encounter in our daily experience. In a certain respect, then, reading is not unlike the practice of science. In science we seek to test our ideas and, when they are confirmed, we experience a considerable source of pleasure. Similarly, it is no less a pleasure when in reading we see ourselves reflected on the page. In both cases there is a delight in the correspondence between a belief about nature or the self, a confirmation that sustains us in our endeavor to make sense of the world in which we live.

Literary truths are not organized as a body of knowledge as they often are in a scientific discipline. They are usually hard to pin down, to remember, and to apply when you might want to, although some are more memorable than others. Yet readers differ widely in what they regard as a literary truth. Additionally, it is often claimed that the truths one finds in literature are unlikely to be found elsewhere.

Its [literature] cultural importance derives…from its success in telling us things about ourselves that we hear from no other quarter.
Salman Rushdie

He liked novels because they dealt with the incommensurable in life, with the things that couldn't

be expressed in any other way.
Richard Ford

We look to fiction for images of reality…that more factual, explanatory accounts cannot quite supply.
John Updike

There may be little disagreement about this once it is recognized that literary and "factual" accounts have entirely different goals. In a recent interview Daniel Gilbert, an experimental social psychologist, commented that "most of what science has to tell us about human behavior already has been divined by writers with great insight."[29] In response to a later question Gilbert admits that there's nothing about "human behavior or the experience of the mind that you cannot find in literature. But on the other hand you can also find the opposite in literature. Everything that can be said about the human condition has been said by some writer." He notes that after reading his most recent book, *Stumbling on Happiness,* where he liberally quotes Shakespeare, a literature professor said, "Given that Shakespeare saw all this stuff, had these insights, why do we need science?" Gilbert replies "Well I could also find ten places where he said exactly the opposite. If you say everything, some of it winds up being right.

The purpose of science then is that it "helps us confirm which writers were right and which were wrong, but it rarely tells us something that a writer of Shakespeare's caliber didn't come up

29   Daniel Gilbert, Powells Bookstore Interview:
      www.powells.com/interviews/danielgilbert.html

with first." But even science, at least the science of human behavior, is stuck with considerable empirical uncertainty. Facts and theories come and go with further research; what is held to be true today will in due course be shown to be false or incomplete or require revision tomorrow. As Gilbert later admits, he always begins his freshman course, Introduction to Psychology, by telling the students "that half of what I teach them will turn out to be wrong; the problem is I don't know which half."

This is precisely what he said about Shakespeare. Indeed, in the psychological sciences the level of inconsistency and disagreement between accounts is scarcely distinguishable from literary accounts. A literary truth is always right, right for its fictional depiction, and right for a reader who finds it expresses something true for them. It may not be true for another reader, let alone many others. But a writer has no designs on formulating general truths, as is the case for science.

The Commonplace Book Tradition

…my diaries, multitude of notebooks and memoranda, box upon box of correspondence and some fragments of memoir. I sift, I file, I collage. I'm trying to set them in some form of order, trying to discern some underlying pattern or theme amidst all that insignificance and muddle. It's a good job for an old man with time on his hands.
William Boyd, *The New Confessions*

A commonplace book is what a provident poet cannot subsist without, for this proverbial reason, that "great wits have short memories": and whereas, on the other hand, poets, being liars by profession, ought to have good memories; to reconcile these, a book of this sort, is in the nature of a supplemental memory, or a record of what occurs remarkable in every day's reading or conversation. There you enter not only your own original thoughts, (which, a hundred to one, are few and insignificant) but such of other men as you think fit to make your own, by entering them there.
Jonathan Swift, *Letter of Advice to a Young Poet*

At the end of this inquiry I return to the questions of whether and how the practice of keeping a commonplace book has changed me. I know it has enhanced my reading experience, as I am sure it has for other readers who keep a similar collection. Reading tends to be a fairly passive process. We move rapidly from sentence to sentence, rarely stopping to mull over any single one. Marking those that seem notable for one reason or another slows reading down. It transforms the reading experience from a page turning exercise into an occasion to think further about the material, while a timely annotation also gives the reader a chance to reflect further on the marked passages and their personal significance. Rarely do we stop to think twice about a passage, or make note of it so that we can react to it sometime later. In my view, this is the real advantage of collecting notable passages. It deepens the reading experience, turns it into an engagement with issues and educational experience.

I have also been wondering how this practice has influenced the beliefs and attitudes I hold. And have I come to a greater understanding of my self as a result of the many long years I have been collecting notable passages from works of literature? I know that I often found a correspondence between my reading and personal experience. But did transcribing the passages that described this relationship change me in anyway? I am sure it has but not in ways that are clearly discernable to me or that I can describe very concretely.

Other than the record keeping itself, I can't think of many activities I engage in now that I would not be doing if I didn't keep a commonplace book. At the same time, I know it has made me into a more alert reader and motivated me to give much more thought to the text than I would if I didn't keep one. Perhaps that has strengthened some of the beliefs and attitudes I hold and led me to think more critically about them. And it has also introduced me to a range of new ideas and to consider their relationship to those I already hold or have come to through other experiences. In the absence of another life or a group of persons to compare with my own experience, the extent of these effects and the specific role of commonplacing in producing them will have to remain a matter of conjecture at this point.

I recall that my initial rationale in making note of dazzling or provocative passages was to learn how to write better. I suspect it has in a limited way. But now I am more focused on collecting ideas. I am sure that has been intellectually worthwhile, at least it has kept me thinking and, above all, identified issues that command my interest and sometimes generate a good deal of further study.

On balance then, the act of transcribing passages surely leaves its mark. While we may be able to assimilate a passage once again by copying it, the fact of the matter is that most commonplace books contain far more entries than any of us can ever hope to recall. So whatever influence the act of copying has, it is surely one that is limited to short-term effects on accessibility and availability. The long-term effects are far weaker. We may recall having read something memorable in a particular book or by a certain author. But unless we go to the effort of memorizing it at the time we transcribe it and perhaps return to it from time to time, we will be hard put to bring forth its content with any confidence.

While I record all these truths in my Commonplace book, these choice pieces of wisdom, I am not at all sure they have a great deal of influence on my day to day behaviors. I often find that they do not readily come to mind when they might be useful. I put these passages to paper in the hope that they will narrow the gap between thought and action and that I will be able to make more intelligent decisions. But I confess that rarely happens.

At a party the other night someone used in jest the phrase "the meaning in life." I instantly recalled reading that very morning a passage in Joseph Epstein's essay *Talking to Oneself* that dealt with the meaning of life.[30] However, while I thought the passage would contribute to our discussion, for the life of me I couldn't recall it. Epstein quotes Edward Shils who, when the son of a friend of his committed suicide leaving a note saying that he found life meaningless, responded: "...of course it is meaningless, but most of us are fortunately too busy to dwell on its meaningless." It was only a few hours before that I had read the essay and had, in fact, copied that very passage into a Word document and then entered it along with a few others from the essay, into my Commonplace Book.

This example is instructive. Most works of literature are usually read in a fairly casual, relaxed fashion. Indeed, some read so quickly it is hard to imagine they are catching much of anything. But for even the most focused readers, it is fair to say that little is recalled or recorded in any permanent fashion. Other than for those who have a photographic memory or are in the practice of regularly reviewing the passages they have collected,

30 Joseph Epstein, *Talking to Oneself.* New Criterion 2001.

it should not be surprising that so very little of what is read is translated into action.

In a review of Keith Gessen's *All the Sad Young Literary Men*, Joyce Carol Oates describes this dilemma well:[31]

> *The predicament of Gessen's characters, as it is likely to be the preeminent predicament of Gessen's generation, is the disparity between what one has learned of history and the possibilities of making use of that knowledge in one's life...*

A lifetime of studying psychology as well a good deal of current research on the many factors that give rise to biases and errors in thinking has convinced me that all too often we overestimate the influence of the written word on behavior. Information by itself, even when it is read carefully and often reviewed does not appear to have a strong effect on behavior. Instead, it represents only one of the many factors that influence behavior, especially in situations where there are other pressures that make it difficult for individuals translate what they have read into action.

The real value, then, of keeping a commonplace book is to insure that whatever it is that we want to remember will permanently reside, not in our mind, but rather in our notebook or computer document, there to revisit and think about further. And by doing so, perhaps we will gradually assimilate these

---

31 Joyce Carol Oates, Youth! *The New York Review of Books*, 55, No. 7, May 1, 2008.

ideas so that they can more readily guide our behavior when they become relevant. Gilbert Highet put it this way: "We are meant to assimilate them as slowly and steadily as a bone grows in our skeleton."[32] But this surely takes much revisiting and a good deal of additional practice.

On Annotating

With rare exceptions I did not annotate the passages at the time they were added to my commonplace book. To annotate takes time. To annotate thoughtfully takes even more time. According to some of the survey respondents annotating also interferes with the flow of ideas and is therefore to be resisted. Indeed, in contrast to historical tradition, the practice of annotating entries in commonplace books has all but disappeared today. Yet on some accounts, it is an essential feature of commonplacing. William Cole claims:

> The key word for the commonplace book is "annotated." It is not just an anthology; the compiler reacts to the passages he has chosen or tells what the passages have led him to think about. A piece of prose, a poem, an aphorism can trigger the mind to consider a parallel, to dredge something from the memory, or perhaps to speculate with further range and depth on the same theme.[33]

Cole leaves open the question of precisely why annotating is so

---

32 op. cit.
33 William Cole. Speaking of Commonplace Books. *New York Times* May, 3, 1970.

important, as well as whether he is referring to annotating each and every passage that one enters in their commonplace book, a task that would take most practitioners several lifetimes to complete. In fact, his definition of the genre—"an annotated personal anthology"—would exclude most of the printed and electronic versions of commonplace books that we know of today. Notable exceptions include in Auden's *A Certain World*, Curtis' *A Commonplace Book* and Cecil's *Library Looking-Glass*, where, in response to a memorable passage, these authors composed brief notes, observations, poems, and sometimes lengthy commentaries.

Linking together similar passages in an extended treatment of their common theme or connections seems to me annotating at its best and most systematic. To paraphrase one of the survey respondents: I am forever searching for inter-connections, for those invisible lines of connection between ideas and things that appear to dwell in mutually exclusive realms. This does not call for a lengthy essay or discourse on the topic at hand, although nothing prevents a reader from composing one. Nor does it call for doing so at the time the passage is read or even when it is entered in a commonplace book. The model I have in mind was described by Olivia Dresher in an e-mail she sent to me:

> So it seems to me that it would be interesting if you were to write an essay in which you moved back and forth from selected quotes which reflect directly on your own experience to explaining how and why they do, talking about your own life and experiences...

And in a way this commentary is an extended annotation on my Commonplace Book entries, a great many of which are cited, in the manner Dresher suggests. It is also an autobiography of the issues that have continued to engage me for a very long now time. Sometimes it takes a fair amount of time for a reaction to a set of passages to develop or for their relationship to come into focus as it did for me in deciding to embark on this analysis.

The Future of Commonplace Books

Will the digital commonplace book replace its written forerunners? There are really two issues implied by this question. The first is the future of electronic transcribing. Will readers come to prefer to record their commonplace selections electronically in a computer document rather than in a hand-written notebook? The second is the degree to which those who keep a commonplace book will wish to make them public. While there will always be readers who prefer to keep their commonplace books in a private hand-written manuscript, it is clear that electronic writing and communication is beginning to reposition commonplacing as a public, communal practice. Perhaps we are entering a transition period where those of us raised to read and write in the traditional fashion will simply fade away and gradually be replaced by those raised to read and write electronically.

Still I wonder. Reading is a largely private activity that often takes place at some distance from a computer. I read in bed, in an armchair, on the terrace, or on a park bench. Countless others do so as well. Who wants to take a computer with them in those settings? In addition, like so many others, I find it extremely difficult to read lengthy documents, including books, on a computer or e-book screen. If it is a short article or essay, I usually print the material; if it's a book or periodical, I purchase a copy.

Some claim there won't be any reason buy a book or print a document as increasingly sophisticated methods of electronic note-taking and reading begin to overcome the barriers to reading and note taking on the computer today. The following scenario was recently described to me in a recent e-mail exchange on this topic:

> *If you could have your book or reading material readable on a device smaller and lighter than a book, yet with your text at any size or degree of sharpness you desire in any degree of bright or dark conditions, if in addition to a single book, this device could hold hundreds of books, even access entire libraries, if the text could be edited, annotated, highlighted, extracted, if the device could be powered by the sun when you are outdoors, by one's own body heat when indoors—in short, if the little device could do anything a larger computer could do only more portably, why would one not want to use it?*[34]

Who can answer a question like this? Fortunately, I will never have to. I find this question somewhat like the one people are

---

34 Victor Munoz. Personal communication. February 14, 2006.

asking about libraries today. Who goes to the library anymore to get a book, let alone read one there? In fact, books are becoming increasingly hard to find in many libraries these days as they have been replaced by row after row of computer stations. But not everything can be read on a computer. And those who undertake serious scholarship will always need to read primary materials. My hunch is that there will always be a reason to go to the library and that there will always be individuals who want to do so. Similarly there will always be readers who find it more congenial and enjoyable to read printed books and to make their notes on paper. There were never very many of us in the first place, but there will always be enough to matter.

Self Analysis

Aside from their basic intellectual or emotional merit, it is also possible to infer from the passages in my Commonplace Book a good deal about my life and personality. As William Cole noted in his article on commonplace books in the *New York Times*: "One gets a pretty good idea of a man, his likes and prejudices, his quirks and manias, the variousness of his mind from reading a commonplace book."[35]

In this respect a person's commonplace book is much like any self-revelatory technique employed in clinical research or practice. Indeed, I have been led to wonder if the practice of copying passages from literature as I have done might have useful psychotherapeutic implications. Consider the routine: clients are asked to mark passages in the books they are reading

35 op.cit.

that seem significant to them and then discusses the reasons they were selected with the therapist.

The notion may seem fanciful, but I am not alone in suggesting it. Just recently I read an observation on this topic by a literature teacher, Edward Santoro that was posted on the web.[36] Santoro wrote:

> *Many years ago I was thinking seriously about a radical psychology (though I wasn't calling it that) that would include fiction as therapy, quite similar to prescribing Prozac or Ritalin or whatever is the flavor of the day. If somebody is trying to work through a difficult issue, particular works of fiction could be prescribed, discussed, analyzed. This dialogue and the learning to think critically about a text would put a person into a better position of knowing the self and society and their interrelation. I thought and still do think this would be a successful therapy. The irony is that this is exactly what education is supposed to do. Years ago I was looking for books on just such a topic, and though there were a few, nothing really described what I had in mind.*

Other than the research applications I have described, there has been no clinical application of this approach as far as I can tell. What I do know is that at times the experience of reading literature can consol me. At other times it provides the kind of insight that traditional therapy is said to offer. In these two

36 http://blog.dennisfox.net/index.php/archives/2004/10/03/literary-therapy

respects, then, reading literary fiction may have some therapeutic effects. Whether it can have the same effects for others in a clinical situation remains an open question at this time.

In rereading some of the passages in my Commonplace Book, it is obvious the way they reflect the continuing concerns and interests that I have. I also found the experience of preparing lists of these passages a rather remarkable one. I kept saying: "No wonder I marked them." More often than not, they were provocative expressions of considerable insight and significance, at times one gem after another. It was often startled to see them on the page again. From my 2007 collection:

> *Never, never did she feel in life the sense of recognition, the companionship, the great warm fact of solidarity that she found between the covers of a book.*

> *Love is letting be. Letting the other be as they are.*

> *...the bond between teacher and student lasts a lifetime...the feelings we have for the teachers or students who have meant the most to us, like those we have for long-lost friends, never go away.*

I also realized that the reasons I may have made note of them many years ago cannot possibly be the ones that draw me to them now. I was much too young then to appreciate the truths that I find in so many of them today. Perhaps my reaction is a simple failure of memory to be sure of the reasons I was intrigued by them originally. Or it might just as readily be due to the multiple ways a passage can be thought of as memorable. Whatever the reason is, I am often surprised to note a comparable regard for a passage that I may have marked in the margin long ago. I also take delight in sensing this continuity in what I regard as worthy of note throughout the many long years of my reading history.

Further, I found a striking consistency in the content of many of the passages recorded for each theme. For example in the passages I recorded on Change, the fourth most frequent category, a sizeable number dealt with the extraordinary difficulty of changing another person's behavior, especially by means of strong external pressures.

> *...essentially you could not persuade anyone to give up something that gave him intense pleasure*
> Joseph Epstein

> *He really didn't believe you could bend others to your will.*
> Jens Christian Grondahl

> *He (Balanchine) was convinced that you could not really change a dancer. All you could do was develop what she already had.*
> Joan Acocella

> *People were always saying something had completely*

changed them, some experience or book or man, but if you knew how they had been before, nothing much really had changed.

James Salter

I also noticed how many I have cited to bolster a point I've made in a lecture or essay I've written. Drawing upon the passages in this way is precisely the way they were used by the scholars and statesmen who kept commonplace books during antiquity and the Renaissance. I suspect the same is also true for present-day writers and teachers who have created commonplace books of their own. Similarly, the commonplace book can become a useful tool in the helping students to develop ideas to write about. Erasmus was among the first to emphasize the considerable value in compiling a commonplace book in the education of young children:

> *I am of this opinion, that young children might muche more to their profecte and benefite bee excercised in the grammar schooles with theme, or arguments to write on...so that the schoolemaister dooe open and declare the rewlis and waies how that which is briefly spoken maye bee dilated and sette out more at large, and how that is fondly spoken...maye bee turned or applied to a serious use and purpose.*

Students often report that one of the greatest hurdles they face in getting started on their writing assignments is in finding ideas to write about. Compiling a collection of topics and themes in their commonplace book might be a valuable tool in helping them to overcome this problem and making them better, more involved readers. A notebook in which they collect notable passages from their reading could easily be drawn upon for writing assignments and might also serve as a catalyst in developing ideas of their own. Recording these passages under appropriate headings is the key to making such a collection useful to students. As Price noted in his discussion of this suggestion: "Without this commonplace book activity, however, very seldom would they take the time to think through ideas and discard insubstantial ones before sitting down to write a complete piece."[37]

Next Steps

This analysis of my Commonplace Book has been more of an exploration than a systematic research project. In terms of future study, the sample selections that I have classified might be completed by examining the pages I omitted. It might also be instructive if another rater replicated my procedure. However, as discussed earlier, there interpretive problems would arise with such a comparison since the experience of other raters would not be the same as mine and thus the meaning and classification of the passages for them would inevitably differ.

The categories were not rigorously defined nor at this stage of my review did I want to stipulate an objective measure of each one. Surely that will be required for any future analysis that intends to be a serious piece of research. Indeed, there is probably considerable overlap between the categories although

37 Gayle B. Price. A case for a modern commonplace book. *College Composition and Communication*, 31, No 2, 175-182. May, 1980.

I tried to reduce that as much as possible as I went along by combining those that were clearly overlapping.

What I have done is admittedly an informal review of my Commonplace Book that scarcely meets the strictures of systematic analysis employed in social research or literary criticism. Instead my goal was to begin to get a sense of what can be done with this kind of material and the kinds of questions one might put to it in a more refined and critical examination.

Commonplace Book Bibliography[38]

W. H. Auden. *A Certain World: A Commonplace Book*, 1970. New York: The Viking Press.

David Cecil. *Library Looking-Glass: A Personal Anthology*, 1975. London: Constable and Company Ltd.

William Cole. "Speaking of Commonplace Books." *New York Times*, May 3, 1970.

Charles P. Curtis. *A Commonplace Book*, 1957. New York: Simon and Schuster.

Robert Darnton. "Extraordinary Commonplaces." *The New York Review of Books*, December 21, 2000.

Benjamin DeMott. "Speaking of Books: Auden's Commonplace Book." *New York Times*, September 13, 1970.

D. J. Enright. *Interplay: A Kind of Commonplace Book*. 1995. New York: Oxford University Press.

---

38 This set of references is confined to works on commonplace books. References related to the subject matter of the chapter topics are footnoted on the page where they are discussed.

Philip Gardner (Ed). *E. M. Forster Commonplace Book*, 1985. Stanford, California: Stanford University Press.

Alec Guiness. *A Commonplace Book*. 2001. London: Penguin Books.

Earle Havens. *Commonplace Books: A History of Manuscripts and Printed Books from Antiquity to the Twentieth Century*, 2001. Lebanon, NH: University Press of New England.

George G. Herrick. *Winter Rules: A Commonplace Book*. 1997. Bethesda, MD: International Scholars Publications.

Gilbert Highet, "Uncommon Thoughts in A Commonplace," *Horizon Magazine*, Vol. IV, September, 1961.

John Locke. *A New Method of a Common-Place Book*, 1706. London.

Ruth Mohl. *John Milton and His Commonplace Book*, 1969. New York: Frederick Ungar Publishing Company.

Ann Moss. *Printed Commonplace-Books and the Structuring of Renaissance Thought*, 1966. New York: Oxford University Press.

Douglas L. Wilson (Ed). *Jefferson's Literary Commonplace Book*, 1989. New Jersey: Princeton University Press.

Other Readings

Waiting for The New Yorker

While the magazine certainly provided some readers with a symbolic city, others saw it as a bastion against the forces of cultural decline.

Mary Corey

The New Yorker was as much a part of our class conditioning as clean fingernails, college, a checking account and good intentions. For better or worse, it probably created our sense of humor.

John Leonard

The New Yorker magazine first drew me to the world of literature and fine writing. To this day and through all its recent transformations, it has continued to play a large role in my literary reading experiences. It is surely the most frequent single source of the entries in my Commonplace Book. I can't be entirely sure when I first started reading *The New Yorker*. Perhaps I was in high school or even younger. But I do recall there was always a copy around the house and I know that once I started reading the magazine, I never stopped. This is a tale told by most dedicated readers, including its current editor, David Remnick, who, upon assuming the post, remarked, "I was raised on this magazine."

What could the magazine have possibly meant to me as a young boy growing up in Los Angeles in the '40s and '50s? I know my mother read it from cover to cover each week, and surely I must have wondered what drew her to those pages with such devotion. No doubt I picked up a copy from time to time, glanced at the articles, and maybe read one or two, perhaps at her suggestion. And then as my education broadened in junior high and then high school, I remember reading sections of the magazine in earnest.

It became my Literature 101: a course that has lasted for years, indeed, to this day. And it introduced me to the cultural life of this country, at least as reflected in the goings on in New York. I became aware of the people who were profiled in the magazine, the heroes of high culture: the books they wrote and films they made or appeared in. I was taken away to worlds I never knew existed by the two or three short stories that were published then in each issue, and by those remarkable letters from foreign cities. What better introduction to Paris than those memorable Letters from Paris by Janet Flanner?

There was even a column on horse racing by Audax Minor, the pen name of George Ryall, which I read with considerable interest since it was not uncommon for my father to take us on the weekend to the thoroughbred races at Hollywood Park or Santa Anita. Imagine that—a column on thoroughbred horse racing in this most hi-brow of magazines. Eventually, it went the way of The Long-Winded Lady, Berton Roueche's Annals of Medicine, and the other little quirks that characterized the magazine, such as the placement of the author's name at the end rather than the beginning of a piece and the absence of a Table of Contents, all of which brought a little mystery to the reading experience. Should I peek at the author's name before I read the story? Should I thumb through the entire issue to learn what's in it? Who could have written this Talk of the Town piece, a question, like the first two, that is no longer required.

More than anything, I think the magazine communicated to me in those early days a standard of discourse and analysis that seemed to be worth emulating. It gave me a model to follow preparing the lectures for my classes and judging the work of others. I wanted to write as clearly and as thoughtfully and occasionally as humorously as the writers did on the pages of *The New Yorker,* and I expected others to do the same. I knew I had a long way to go, but *The New Yorker* pointed the way for me. In that respect, nothing has changed in the ensuing years.

In May of 2000, the magazine held a festival in New York to celebrate its 75th Anniversary. Many of its well-known authors read from their work, some lectured, and others participated in panel discussions or gave interviews. The New Yorker Festival was such a success that it has been repeated every year since. Think of it: the writers of a weekly magazine holding forth about their work during three full days of readings, lectures, and discussions. Outside academic society meetings, I can think of nothing else like it in this country, surely not by any other magazine or periodical. When I went to the Festival the following year, I was surprised by the large crowds at most of the events and the fact that, while most were from New York

City, a goodly number had come from distant locations. I had traveled across the country from Oregon; one woman I met had come all the way from Honolulu.

What led me and so many others to travel so far, at some expense, to attend this Festival? More than anything, I think we came to make contact with a few of its talented contributors and to connect in some vague fashion with the community of readers and writers who recognize the unique and special value of the magazine. Many of its most notable contributors were present the year I attended. On Fiction Night, which opened the Festival, I had to choose between Anne Beattie and Richard Ford, or Michael Cunningham and Deborah Eisenberg, or Nick Hornby and Zadie Smith, or Lorrie Moore and Julian Barnes, and other pairs no less notable. The choice was impossible. The seminars and presentations on each of the following two days were no less impressive.

David Remnick's interview of Woody Allen was far and away the most popular event of the Festival the year I attended. A huge room in the New York Public Library was used for the session. Woody ambled in and the crowd roared. Remnick, who seemed to be everywhere at the Festival, reported that the session sold out the day tickets went on sale. Woody admitted he was not a scholar, saying he is just Woody and everyone loved his modest, unassuming, and fun-loving self-deprecation. He's a natural at it and good at poking fun at much of modern life, without annoying anyone. He loves to write, hates leaving his apartment, and doesn't care what people say about his work; he just needs to do it. Otherwise, he would collapse. Woody offered an interesting view of greatness: you do what you do, you do what you do best, and if others like it or think it's great, then that's fine. And if they don't, that's fine too. But you always have to do what you like to do and what you do naturally. Talent is a gift, not something you can try to attain. You can work at perfecting it, but first it has to be there.

The arrival of *The New Yorker* is one of the main events of my week. It bothers me when it isn't delivered on time, and if it doesn't arrive the next day or so, I will go out to buy a copy at the newsstand. Of course, it usually drifts in the day after that. But I'd rather not run the risk that it won't, or, as happens now and then, that it will be delivered by mistake to someone else.

With the exception of the recently introduced double issues, the magazine has been published every week for the past eighty-three years. Frankly, I find this rather astonishing. Putting together a magazine of this quality *week after week* for as many years as that (with no reason to believe it will be any different in the years ahead) seems something of a miracle to me.

You have to stand before the bound volumes of the magazine on the shelves of any major library to really appreciate why I say this. When I found myself doing this the other day, I was dumbfounded by the row upon row of back issues of the magazine. Then, as I began my search for the Talk of the Town piece I wanted to cite, I realized I was going through one issue after another, as though it was the latest. Hours later, I found the piece I was seeking, although it would have taken but a moment had I had not been so caught up in thumbing through the old issues page by page.

Everything was still there. The advertisements for fashionable clothes and exotic places, the hilarious cartoons, the profiles of people-you-always-wanted-to-meet. The essays were longer then, but no less serious, and once they captured your interest, they took forever to finish. The same was true of the Profiles, the Letters posted from European capitals or those unforgettable Pauline Kael film reviews, none of which seemed the least bit dated on rereading.

There were more short stories then and who would not want to re-read those that moved you the first time around; Cheever's "The Country Husband", Salinger's "A Perfect Day for Bananafish", William Maxwell's "What He Was Like", or Munro's "The Jack Randa Hotel". Here still is classic literature about memorable people and situations that continue to bring pleasure and personal insights that you had not recognized before.

I can clearly recall the first time I read some of those stories and how I was affected by the experience. To cite an instance, I will never forget the first time I read "The Jack Randa Hotel," Munro's comedic tale of a fractured marriage and runaway husband. It was late in the afternoon, the day was warm, and I was in Italy, on the rooftop terrace of the hotel in Florence where I was staying. It was a *perfect moment*. I read her story slowly, very slowly, as I knew the moment would not last long or be repeated soon, if ever, again.

Like other longtime readers, I go through each issue in a fairly regular fashion. I turn at once to the Table of Contents, also a recent addition, to learn who the writers are and on what subject they have written. Then I proceed, page by page, through the entire issue for the first time, reviewing the Talk of the Town, the cartoons, the poems, occasional side-bars, and the ads, especially the little ones which appear in column format toward the end of the issue. After a suitable period of restraint, I commence reading a fair amount of each issue.

With few exceptions, I have been doing this every week for more than fifty years. Recently I have begun to wonder about the cumulative impact of this experience. How has this steady diet of reading *The New Yorker* influenced the life I lead or the work I do? Granted, this is a difficult question; I'm not sure it can ever be answered. Yet, in a way, isn't it the kind of question we might ask of any aesthetic or intellectual experience? How do the films we see, the books we read, or the theatrical events we attend influence us? These questions have always been difficult to answer.

But a lifelong experience of reading *The New Yorker* is not very different from those experiences and must surely leave an imprint upon its readers. Without any systematic research, there are two approaches one can take in trying to identify the nature of this influence. One can either imagine what a regular reader's life would be like without the magazine or, alternatively, recount in a concrete way how the magazine has shaped the actions they take and beliefs they hold. The first approach would yield a fairly speculative account; in fact, it would probably lead to several. So instead, I will adopt the second by considering my own experience, since *The New Yorker* continues to have a prominent place in my life.

As I begin to think about this matter, I realize that I read the magazine much the way I read most written materials. I make comments in the margins, copy notable passages, and duplicate articles that I want to save. An article has more than once motivated me to read more on a topic, undertake a research project, or turned my interests in a new direction. I often talk about the articles with friends and students. Some, like John Hersey's *Hiroshima* or Rachel Carson's *Silent Spring* and, more recently, Malcolm Gladwell's work on the *Tipping Point,* have spurred me to action and debate. I will often cite a *New Yorker* essay in the writing I do, and, from time to time, refer to them in the lectures I give.

In my social psychology class, to cite one instance, I often lecture about the effects of violence in the media. The students are always interested in the research on this issue, even if it is inconclusive. In preparing the lecture, I look over the material in my file each year to incorporate the latest studies and review those that I have found the most instructive. In doing so, I always re-read Pauline Kael's masterly review of "Bonnie and Clyde" that appeared in the October 21, 1967 issue.

My first thought, of course, is that no one writes movie reviews with that kind of brilliance any more. But I don't speak about that with the students. Instead, I discuss her analysis of the role of violence in the film, and show how it anticipated future research findings on the impact of media violence. Kael wrote:

> *Such people [those who want to place legal restraints on movie violence] see "Bonnie and Clyde" as a danger to public morality; they think an audience goes to a play or a movie and takes the actions in it as examples for imitation. They look at the world and blame the movies. But if women who are angry with their husbands take it out on the kids, I don't think we can blame "Medea" for it; if, as has been said, we are a nation of mother-lovers, I don't think we can place the blame on "Oedipus Rex."*

> *The movies may set styles in dress or love-making, they may advertise cars or beverages, but art is not examples for imitation... people don't "buy" what they see in a movie quite so simply; Louis B. Mayer did not turn us into a nation of Andy Hardys, and if, in a film, we see a frightened man want only to take the life of another, it does not encourage us to do the same, any more than seeing an ivory hunter shoot an elephant makes us want to shoot one. It may, on the contrary, so sensitize us that we get a pang in the gut if we accidentally step on a moth."*

There is always a lively discussion after I read these passages, each of which makes an important point about the purported effects of exposure to film violence. This, in turns, gives me a chance to discuss current research on her claims. Kael's analysis brings our discussion of media violence into contact with the actual film-going experience of individuals who are thought to be influenced one way or another by violent films. This contrasts with the artificial nature of most laboratory studies in this area. Regrettably, because they support the views of those who wish to regulate the media, they are the ones most frequently cited in public policy discussions of this issue.

Every now and then, after mulling over a *New Yorker* piece, I will want to look further into a topic it has considered. That was certainly true in the case of Meghan Daum's article, "Virtual Love", that appeared in the August 25, 1997 issue, almost thirty years after Kael's review. Daum's essay, which the magazine placed in its "Brave New World Department", vividly recounts the reactions of a young woman to a romance that had originated on the Internet. It was not a happy experience, although when it began, Daum was instantly caught up in the "exhilaration" of digital courtship. She wrote:

> *But, curiously, the Internet felt anything but dehumanizing. My interaction with PFSlider seemed more authentic than much of what I experienced in the daylight realm of living beings. I was certainly putting more energy into the relationship than I had put into many others."*

Her essay led me to wonder about the features of electronic communication that might make it so easy to form online relationships, and whether these relationships differed from those established in the usual ways. I began by investigating the prevalence and durability of cyber-relationships. Daum reports that:

...at least seven people confessed to me the vagaries of their own E-mail affairs...This topic arose, unprompted, in the course of normal conversation. ...we all shook our heads in bewilderment as we told our tales...These were normal people, writers and lawyers and scientists. They were all smart, attractive, and more than a little sheepish about admitting just how deeply they had been sucked in. Mostly, it was the courtship ritual that had seduced us. E-mail had become an electronic epistle, a yearned-for rule book. It allowed us to do what was necessary to experience love.

At the time, nothing was known about the frequency of cyber-romances. To find out, I surveyed over 1,000 students with Internet accounts at a nearby university and was surprised to learn that thirty-six per cent of those who responded indicated they had formed a close friendship with another individual in an online setting. Twenty-two per cent described it as a close romantic relationship. Even more surprising was the finding that, like Daum, the students did not characterize their on-line relationships as shallow or distant. Quite to the contrary, they claimed to have formed genuinely close friendships that were every bit as satisfying as those established in traditional ways. In fact, in some instances, they had led to marriage.

Most of the week I do research or devote myself to teaching. In either case, the subject matter almost always has something to do with psychology, primarily social or environmental. I am drawn by the relevance of these areas to everyday life. At times the research does capture my interest; occasionally it will even surprise me; but most of the time it does neither. Above all, it never fulfills a longing I seem to have for something of artistic or literary merit or something that emotionally gives me pause.

More often than not, *The New Yorker* comes to my rescue. There I find the culture that is absent from my ordinary world, and ideas that often seem truer than the ones I encounter in psychology. When I see the magazine in the mailbox, I must confess to being more than a little bit grateful that it has once again come my way. I welcome it like a close friend who stops by for a visit each week. *The New Yorker*, as former editor William Shawn put it, seems like "…an oasis…in a period in which so much of life is debased and corrupted."[39] Yes, that is it precisely, even truer now than it was when he said it.

I know my *New Yorker* is not everyone's *New Yorker*. But in reading the magazine each week, I have come to feel part of the community of other readers who value polished writing and serious commentary. The symbolic nature of this community makes it no less real. In *The World Through a Monocle*,[40] Mary Corey captured this bond quite well: "Some felt a profound kinship with the magazine because it spoke for them, giving a public voice to their own private intelligences. It says "what I

---

39 Cited in an unpublished paper, *We're Not Making For Automobiles! Writing, Reading and Professional Identity at the New Yorker*, presented by Trysh Travis at the Modern Language Association Meeting, 1996.

40 Mary F. Corey, *The World Through a Monocle: The New Yorker at Midcentury*, 1999. Cambridge: Harvard University Press.

think and feel," a Washington, D.C. woman wrote, "as I should like to have said it."

In a sense, *The New Yorker* has become my "Third Place"—a term coined by Ray Oldenberg to refer to those informal gathering places in the community that an individual is drawn to each day outside of their home and workplace. French cafes, English pubs and Italian piazzas are such places. I do not have a Third Place that I am drawn to at the end of the day. Indeed, I do not believe there are many such gathering places in this country.

However, through *The New Yorker,* I find a group of like-minded regulars who have come together for informal discussion and thoughtful banter and where someone can always be counted on for good story or an idea worth considering. I go in solitude and, while I can't converse with them later, in other settings, I can speak with others about the "discussion" that I have overheard at *The New Yorker.*

This is the kind of special relationship that is said to develop between *The New Yorker* and its readers, and the way in which the magazine has sustained and educated me during all the years that I have been a reader. One of the respondents to Ben Yagoda's recent survey of dedicated *New Yorker* readers recalled an experience she had while serving as a nurse during World War II in a remote section of northern Italy.[41] She reported being asked by a wounded soldier, "If you could have

41 Ben Yagoda, *About Town: The New Yorker and the World It Made,* 2000. New York: Scribner.

anything right now, what would it be?" In an instant she replied, "An issue of *The New Yorker* magazine," whereupon the two—wounded soldier and American nurse, in that far off time and place—began reminiscing about their favorite *New Yorker* cartoons and writers. Deserted island, northern Italian hospital: I can't imagine responding any differently.

A Table in the Stacks

The library in the middle of the campus was as cool as a cave and nearly empty in July. It was in places like this—solemn and welcoming, high and dim and paneled in dark wood and going on in many directions—-that Kit's dreams often took place.
John Crowley, The Translator

It is rare to find a commonplace book in even the finest bookstores or the Web in an electronic version. Instead, to read a published commonplace book, you have to place an order for it and hope that it is still in print or visit a nearby library that may, again if you are lucky, have one or two volumes. However, to read most of the really interesting contemporary and historically important commonplace books or any of the rare and largely unknown treasures of the Classical and Renaissance eras, you really have to go to one of the major university libraries in the United States or Europe.

While I've never been able to visit any of these collections, I have had the good fortune to spend a large portion of my life in several much-loved libraries stretching back to the very early days of my youth. During World War II in the neighborhood where I lived, a small lending library of current fiction and non-fiction books was maintained in a nearby home. Anyone could pay a modest fee to borrow a book for a week or so, making it unnecessary to purchase a copy or wait until one because became available at the distant public library. It wasn't so easy to buy books during those wartime years so the little lending library around the block became a popular and much appreciated neighborhood center. Whatever happened to those small private lending libraries? Outside of New York, I suspect they have all but vanished from this country.

About the time I entered Junior High, I began to study at the Beverly Hills Library. It was a small library located in the City Hall of what was then a village, albeit no less fashionable than now. The library was not far from my home and eventually I began biking or taking the bus there several times a week. It was quiet. The tables were hidden from one another in between the open stacks that filled the rooms. The books that I needed then were readily available. But mostly I would go to study and read. It was more than enough to simply be amongst those books for an hour or two in the afternoon.

I recall an older man was always there when I arrived. Now that I think about it, he must have been about the same age as I am now. Perhaps he was a writer for he was always scribbling something diligently on a pad of yellow paper. I recall being impressed by his devotion to his craft and the seriousness of intent. Strangely, after all of these years, I've not forgotten him or that strange blend of paper, leather, and dust that I inhaled each time I stepped foot in the little library on the second floor of the Beverly Hills City Hall.

Since then I have been to many fine libraries: Widener, Bodleian, the libraries at Stanford and Berkeley. I am overwhelmed with gratitude each time I step foot in one of these places. The first time I wandered in to the great reading room of the New York Public Library I had to stop and catch my breath. Before me were row upon row of tables with hundreds of readers peering at their books. I walked down one of the long aisles lined with book shelves, glimpsing the titles of reference books, most of which I didn't even know existed, crossed over to the other side that housed a comparable collection that I would love to be able to get my hands on now. It was hard to leave. While I usually work alone in my study, after being in that room, I realized for perhaps the first time that I could actually read and write in the reading room of the New York Public Library and that if I lived in New York, I would probably go there every day. I can't imagine a better reason to move there.

And yet, in spite of the resources of the New York Public Library and other comparable collections, the Beverly Hills Library, like any first love, will always remain my favorite. It is where I would want to be when it becomes time to read my last book. I am sure the card catalogue will still be there. After all, the librarians at the Beverly Hills Library would never think of abandoning it for something as racy as a computer.

I met my wife in the library at Stanford. She claims she saw me studying in the main reading room. She recalls I was wearing khaki pants and a tweed sport coat, with my feet propped up on the table. She said I looked like an interesting person, an impression that turned out to be woefully off the mark. Be that as it may, I often wonder if we would have ever met if the library had been nothing more than a room full of digital workstations?

Early in my freshman year at Stanford I began working at the Library. In those days the great collection of books in the stacks was not open to the students. At the circulation desk I would receive the student request card, try to recall on what level the book's call number was located, head into the stacks, down the stairs, through the long and dark aisles, until I came to the right shelf, run my hand along the spine of the books, glancing from time to time at the titles, wishing I could stop to read one or two, scanning the Dewey Decimal numbers, collect the book if it was there, head back down the aisle, up the stairs and pass the book on to the staff to be checked out after stealing a glance at its introductory pages.

That sounds pretty tedious. It wasn't. I liked wandering around the shelves, always intrigued by the books that were stored there, the new topics and areas of study that I didn't know existed, stopping every now and then to grab a book to bring upstairs to read until I had to head down again to fetch another. Eventually I became eligible for one of the study tables located on each floor of the stacks. There I could keep my textbooks and other volumes that I had checked out from the library and do my class work in a setting that is about as favorable as they come. I spent most of my days and many nights at that table in the stacks of the Stanford Library. It was utterly peaceful there, no one else was around and I could come and go whenever I pleased. Since I was in the throes of academic discovery, it was the best of all possible places.

And so I have mixed feelings about the news that Google is embarking on a major program to add the contents of the books in the world's major libraries to its database. The librarian at Stanford, Michael Keller, predicted: "Within two decades, most of the world's knowledge will be digitized and available, one hopes for free reading on the Internet…" Later he went on to dispute the claim that once this is done it will make the "physical books redundant." "I disagree," he said. "In fact, I believe having books in digital form will actually increase the use of the physical books. The digital files will be great for searching and targeting material for study, but many of us prefer the hard copy original in hand for careful reading."[42]

Yes, that may be true for his generation and mine, but I am led to wonder if it will also be true for the generations raised in the digital world. Why would anyone want to want to go to the library to read a book when it can be read anywhere online? Who will need to go to the library when that happens? I imagine there will still be many good reasons to buy books, from the simple pleasures of having them nearby, to preserving and collecting them and, in my case, making notes in the margins and inside cover. Is there anything more annoying than taking a book out of the library only to find that a previous reader or several have made extensive comments and underlines throughout the text?

In the old days, we went to the library to find a book; now it can be ordered online and be at your doorstep the next day. With

42 Michael Keller, *Stanford Alumni Magazine,* Spring 2005.

increasing frequency books can now be read (or listened to) by downloading an electronic version to the computer or portable music player. In the old days we went to the library to read a back issue of a periodical; many are now on the Web and can be read with a couple of clicks. Look how easy it is. Go to Google, type the title of the report, scroll down the search results, click on the title shown in the search result page, bingo there it is, print and staple, all in a flash. Now it is articles and reports. Soon it will be books and entire libraries. Even the venerable New York Public Library has placed online its "collection of prints, maps, posters, photographs, illuminated manuscripts, sheet-music covers, dust jackets, menus and cigarette cards."[43] Is this how Google and the other library digitizers are going to empty out the great reading rooms of the world?

In a recent essay, *The New Yorker's* film critic, David Denby, writes about Susan Sontag's devotion to the cinema. He refers to her essay, *A Century of Cinema,* that in light of Denby's praise, I wanted to read. Naturally I began Googling it. No luck. The complete article, originally published in *Frankfurter Rundschau* in 1995, did not show up on any of Google's citations, although it was referred to several times. Denby also said that a shorter version had been reprinted in the *New York Times.* So I did a search on the *Times'* website. It duly informed me that my search for *A Century of Cinema* by Susan Sontag returned 0 results in all fields.

It was clear what I had to do. I had to get on the bus, go down

---

43 *New York Times* March 03, 2005.

to the library, track down the 1995, issue of *Franfurter Rundschau* and read the original article itself in the library's bound volume of the journal. Fortunately, I still knew how to do that. In a word, far from everything is on the Web. And it is hard to imagine that all the print materials, the books, the journals, the documents in all the libraries scattered throughout the world will ever be digitized. There will always be a goodly sum of materials that will never find their way to the Web.

Even if they do, isn't the central issue the benefits of using print materials for detailed research and analysis, behaviors that are not readily carried out online, at least in my experience? Maybe the younger generation, raised on computers in a way I was not, is able to do so. But I am dubious and am growing increasingly concerned that students are simply not willing or able to conduct the kind of comprehensive literature search and subsequent analysis that I was taught to carry out with books that I found in the library.

The other day I received word of an experiment conducted by a graduate student that virtually replicated one I had done several years ago. I wanted to find out if my study was discussed or even referenced by the student. In due course, I received a pre-publication copy of his study from a colleague over the Internet, to be sure. I searched in vain for any mention of my study or its citation in the set of references. My study has been widely cited and is barely twelve years "old." Surely it would appear in even a casual bibliographic search of the topic. Yes, this is a single example but the claim that students are getting lazy about their research, especially bibliographic research, is one I often hear expressed by academic colleagues and professional librarians.

Is anyone going to the library now? To find out I went over to the Portland State University library the other day. I walked in the main entry and was immediately confronted by a room full of computers, with a student working at each console and a long line of other students waiting for an opening. I counted about fifty workstations and as I walked up and down row upon row of workstations. I failed to see a single person reading a book. Some were taking notes from a website, others were writing text, while still others were composing e-mails. I went upstairs and observed much the same at about a dozen round tables each with five radiating computer stations, fully occupied with students peering at the screen.

As far as I could tell, no one was reading from a book. Where were the books, anyway? What a barren place, I thought. Off to the side there were a few scattered readers. Most of them were taking notes from textbooks, not anything from the library collection. However, I did see a fair number of students listening intently to their iPods and talking enthusiastically on their cell phones.

Up to the third, fourth and fifth floor with progressively fewer students but almost without exception each one working away on their laptops. These floors were largely devoted to the library's open stacks, aisle after aisle of book shelves crammed full of books, journals, and monographs. I walked down the central aisle of each floor, glancing to my left and then to my right and I did not see a single individual browsing through these books. I did see a few library personal returning books to the shelves. That was reassuring. And there were a small number of students reading at the largely empty tables on the perimeter of each floor, but not one by a pile of books that they had collected from the stacks or checked out from the library. So many books, so many unopened, untouched books, so few, if any, readers year after year.

Still, more and more books are being printed each year. The number of library books in circulation is not growing in tandem, as most librarians report that their circulation figures are holding steady or decreasing. In contrast, electronic usage has increased significantly with a dramatic raise in "hits" to library electronic databases. Another result of the digital revolution is the allocation of library funds with a major shift away from books to electronic resources. As a case in point, in 1998, the library at the University of Texas in Austin spent roughly five per cent of its annual materials budget on electronic resources and thirty per cent on monographs. In only three years, those allocations have been reversed so that in 2001 twenty per cent was spent on electronic materials and only fifteen per cent on monographs.[44] Virtually every library in this country reports comparable trends.

Library response to their increasingly serious book storage problem is another sign of their transformation by the digital age. New library designs, as well as renovations of older ones,

44 *The Library Journal,* September 1, 2001.

call for storing books in buildings apart from the library computer centers. A major renovation at the University of Minnesota-Twin Cities library removed the books from the stacks and relocated them to the basement or elsewhere on the campus, to provide space for computer labs and a digital media center. The University of Texas recently moved all of it 90,000-volume collection from the main library to other areas of the campus to open up the area for a "twenty-four hour electronic information commons." This increasingly widespread trend will make it more and more difficult to actually obtain printed volumes. One member of Marquette Universities Library Planning Committee commented: "Despite everyone's best efforts, it will signal to the students that books and journals are old-fashioned, and that computers and the World Wide Web and e-learning are modern and up-to-date."[45]

It seems inevitable that libraries will cease to be places where we go to find the books we would like to read, or to search for others we would like to review. Indeed, they will no longer be there. The new bookless libraries will cease to be "a place in which literary and artistic materials such as books, periodicals, newspapers, pamphlets, prints, records, and tapes, are kept for reading, reference or lending."[46] Nor will they be centers of book collections where students and faculty go because of the sheer pleasure of being there, to inhale the old paper and the leather bindings, or to run into an old friend or one whom you might like to befriend. Instead, they will become buildings full of computers, media centers, and other electronic gadgetry. Those who are there will devote themselves to database

45 *The Chronicle of Higher Education,* July 12, 2002.

searches, reading text on small rectangular screens, and preparing their next PowerPoint presentation.

What will be gained and lost by the digital transformation of libraries? When I was studying at my table in the stacks during undergraduate days, every once in a while, I'd take a little "study break" to wander up and down the aisles to check the titles of the books that caught my eye. This kind of exploration will no longer be possible in the new bookless library. There will be no discovery of that unknown book that you subsequently find indispensable. Thomas Benton has recently described the importance of such moments in the process of doing research.

> *I remember one time I was writing about Edgar Allan Poe and phrenology when I found a box of ephemera— not catalogued in any detail—that included a pamphlet for a book by an early psychologist who analyzed Poe on the basis of daguerreotypes of the poet. I quickly found the book in another area of the same library, and discovered a sequence of pages that purported to show that Poe was suffering from a disorder that affected only one hemisphere of his brain and that revealed itself in the asymmetry of his face...that accidental discovery—the centerpiece of a subsequent article— would never have been made but for the serendipity and convenience of the stacks.*[46]

How often I recall a similar experience in my own research in

46 Thomas H. Benton, "Stacks Appeal." *Chronicle of Higher Education,* July 18, 2005.

the library. I would go in search of a particular bound volume of a journal. Accidentally I'd pick out the wrong volume and begin scanning the pages only to discover another article, perhaps even more important than the one I was searching for and that, in turn, led me on a path of further inquiry that would never haved occurred if I had searched for the article online. Who has not had the pleasure of discovering such an article by thumbing through the journals of their discipline?

To be sure searching on line can be a rich source of information and unexpected sources do appear sometimes. But the search is a targeted one, a rather narrow one. You are looking for a particular document and you find it or something close. As a friend wrote to me in describing her own online experiences: "There is no room in that equation for the serendipitous discovery. When all goes well, you find what you are looking for. But sometimes what you need to find is what you are not looking for."

A few months ago I went back to the library to try to locate the date of an article in *The New Yorker* that I had copied many years ago. Fortunately, the bound volumes of the magazine that has been published week after week since 1925 were still on the shelves in the stacks. I thought for more than a moment about the remarkable treasures contained within those pages. And then I wondered what will become of all those volumes in the new bookless library? I do know that every page of every issue of the Magazine from February 1925 through April 2007 is now available on a portable hard drive. I guess that will settle the matter—no more going to the library; instead load the hard drive and start reading. However, I also know that will never provide the pleasure of thumbing through those well-worn, slightly yellowing pages of the Magazine found on the shelves of the libraries of yesteryear.

The only places where the traditional library seems alive are the private subscription or lending libraries, not unlike the little neighborhood lending library where my mother worked for a while during World War II. Most of these venerable institutions are located in the United Kingdom. However, one of the most notable is The Society Library in New York City, which to my mind remains what an ideal library might be if one could create one from scratch. Part club, part collection of books, part haven for writers and readers since 1754, David Halberstam writes that the Society Library is really more of a "sanctuary than a library."[47]

According to Halberstam, the library has become a place for writers to gather and work by themselves without being entirely by themselves. He says: "I don't necessarily talk to them and they don't necessarily talk to me, but for the moment I feel a little less alone." Wendy Wasserstein said she has done much of her writing there. "The Society Library is an almost perfect place to work: it is pleasant, it is quiet, it has a surprising number of books that you may want and it is genteel. Besides the neighborhood is filled with a number of good places for a late lunch…" What writer or reader has not

47 David Halberstam, *The New York Times,* December 19, 1997.

dreamed that there was such an old fashioned library in their neighborhood?

I have always wanted to be able to join a library club like the New York Society Library. To the best of my knowledge there are only a few of its kind in this country, none of which are located in the town where I live. A private reading/discussion club has always been my model of a third place—quiet rooms to read, others to write, and still others for good conversation. That would be a library at its best. Warm wood-paneled walls of bookcases, row after row of richly-bound volumes, with their "intoxicating mixture of vellum, paper and dust"[48]—this is the library of my youth, the library that is one by one fading away, overcome by the digital revolution. One wonders if it will also carry away respect for the culture of serious scholarship that it sustains.

One night recently I went to the university library again hoping to find some recent journal articles that I couldn't locate on the Web. I arrived about 7 pm. The place seemed empty. I went down to the basement to locate the first journal. I had been misinformed. The library didn't have it. Most of the lights were out. It seemed very dark. I thought there must have been a power outage or an electrical problem. I hiked up to the fifth floor to find the next journal. The volume I wanted was missing. The lights were out up there, as well. Down to the second floor for the last one. It wasn't on the shelf either. But I found another with an interesting report. Down to the first

48 Ben Macintyre, Paradise is Paper, Vellum and Dust. *London Times Online*, December 18, 2004.

floor to copy it. No. The copy room was closed. Eventually I realized that the entire library was closed. It had been closed all the while I was there. They were about to lock up the place. How delightful, I thought, to be locked up in the library with all those books and journals all night.

Journey Through the Book

Culture is not only passed on orally or by instinctive imitation, but above all through reading and study, hence also through the assistance of such a small object as a bookmark.
Marco Ferreri, *Bookmarks*

While only a few readers place marks in the margin by the notable passages they find on the page, almost all mark their place in a book in some fashion when they put the book down. I had forgotten about the special nature of this practice until from out of the blue a friend recently sent me a beautiful book on the subject of bookmarks.[49] What an unusual subject for a book, I thought. The small volume is much like a catalogue that you would find at a museum. In fact, it was published in conjunction with a bookmark exhibition held in Milan a few years ago that was organized by Italian furniture manufacturer.

Again I thought how strange that seemed—what do bookmarks have to do with manufacturing furniture? However, the author assured me that a furniture manufacturer's interest in bookmarks should not appear the least bit odd by pointing out that the tables and chairs that his firm makes are closely

49 Marco Ferreri. (1995). *Bookmarks*. Corraini Editore: Mantova, Italy

associated with the act of reading and studying, both of which require that a bookmark be close at hand. Who can deny such impeccable logic?

Each page of the book displays a collection of bookmarks reproduced in their approximate size and color and organized around a common theme— bookshops, publishers, cinemas, propaganda, cosmetics, etc. I had no idea there were so many different varieties of bookmarks or that they were often crafted with such artistic skill. The book is a work of art in itself, and it started me mulling over the role that bookmarks play in my own reading life, and then, the more I dwelled on it, what they mean for readers in general.

I don't know if you feel the same, but I'm very particular about the bookmarks I use. They have to be just the right size. I don't like small ones like the business cards or bus tickets that some readers use; they tend to fall out of books or get lost somewhere, so they are really quite useless. I don't much care for paper clips that crease the pages of the books I am reading or those printed on flimsy paper that tear or bend easily. The bookmarks at Powell's in Portland, Oregon, said to be one of the world's largest bookstores, used to be like that. I never liked them at all and always put them in my recycling box whenever I found one in a book I had purchased there. But Mr. Powell must have taken to heart comparable stories from his many loyal customers for just recently I noticed he has stiffened up his bookmarks so that they now remain in the books I buy there, rather than on the stack of papers in my recycling box.

One of my favorite bookmarks is given out by a small, independent bookstore in Portland that I've been going to for almost 40 years. It is a miracle the store is still in business, given the likes of Amazon.com and the crowd at Borders and Barnes & Noble. The store is called Twenty-Third Avenue Books, and they have an almost perfect bookmark, one that has remained the same during all the years that I've been going there. They keep doling them out from an inventory that must number in the millions.

They are just the right size, about five inches long, and just the right texture, firm and not easily bent. It would not surprise me if I still had some of the very first they gave to me. Their address and phone number are printed on one side, while on the other is a quote by A. Edward Newton: "The buying of more books than one can read is nothing less than the soul reaching toward...infinity." Nothing fancy, just the basics, along with a suggestion about how to help them stay in business. I am also partial to their bookmarks (I never throw one away) because I like the bookish atmosphere in the store, the people who work there, and the fact that it is still operating after all these years and all the changes that have taken place in the neighborhood and the book-selling business.

Some of the books I like to read are reviewed in *The New York Times* or one of the other literary publications I've been reading lately. If it is thoughtful analysis, I will print a copy, fold it into bookmark shape, and keep it to use as a bookmark in my copy of the book. This makes a dandy bookmark, one that I can review from time to time as I read the book. Not colorful or the least bit artistic, but definitely informative, as well as functional. I seem to be using them more and more lately, which is too bad for all the bookmark artists and printers hard at work at their trade.

Every now and then I read a book that is a treasure. Some of these are reference books, like the dictionary or encyclopedia. Others are books of paintings or photographs. These books clearly require one of the cherished bookmarks that I've collected over the years in my travels. These usually turn out to be made of thin leather with a calligraphed message or distinctive symbol printed on the front side. Or the book might already include one of those colorful ribbon strips that sometimes accompany those really fine and important books, as well as all my red Michelin guides of hotels and restaurants in Italy and France.

These narrow cloth or silk ribbons that are bound into the book at the top of the spine are said to be the eighteenth and nineteenth century precursors of the modern bookmark. It is a mystery why they aren't included in every book. Wonder of wonders, the *Paris Review* now includes a bookmark with each issue. Such a simple idea—promote the periodical, aid those who take their time reading the material, point the way to the publisher's website where the reader can search the archive, listen to poems, and by golly also subscribe. Then again, maybe it is not such a good idea, since if it is widely adopted, it will likely be the end of bookmark craftsman, as well as the pleasure of collecting distinctive bookmarks.

I keep my most valued bookmarks in a very special box upon

my desk. My wife, who knows all too well how keen I am about nifty boxes, gave it to me on one of my birthdays one year. The box is about the size of an egg carton, opens with a hinged lid, and has always sat upon my desk ever since I received it. It has more than enough room to house all my favorite bookmarks. The lid is appropriately calligraphed with passages about writing.: "*Writing is nothing more than a guided dream* (Jorge Luis Borges). *If there's a book you really want to read, but it hasn't been written yet, then you must write it* (Toni Morrison). *True ease in writing comes from art not chance* (Proust)."

Most of the special bookmarks that I place in this box are from Italy, some are from Oxford, and a couple that I still have are from the Library of Congress. I also keep at least one from my favorite bookstores—Kepler's in Menlo Park, Cody's in Berkeley, Blackwell's in London, WH Smith in Paris, and Powell's, just down the block from my home. I also keep one made by the publisher of a little book of essays that I wrote. This bookmark has a blurb about the book and a photograph of me with my cat, Ernie, sitting on my shoulders. Silly, isn't it? These bookmarks do more than allow me to mark my place in a book. They also set loose a string of associations about the places I visited, who I was with, what the weather was like, and what I did when I was there, or, in the case of the bookmark for my recent book, the pleasure I had in writing those essays.

One of the principal rules of bookmarking use is that the book and its bookmark must be suitably matched. You wouldn't want to use a bookmark from Twenty-Third Avenue Books in the

Second Edition of the *American Heritage Dictionary* or the *Collected Photographs of Edward Steichen*. Books like those call for one of those special leather bookmarks with the calligraphed text and striped bottom edge.

I've asked a few of my reader friends if they have any special preference about the bookmarks they use. One reported she uses any old item that happens to be hanging around, like an old post card, Polaroid, or food stamp pamphlet. Another wrote to me that she never leaves a bookstore without checking to see if they have a bookmark to add to her rather enormous collection. She reported that, aside from bookstores, her best finds are in museums. She is also particular about her bookmarks, noting that she doesn't really like the metal or plastic versions because they don't feel quite right. Who wants to keep a lump of metal in the middle of a book?

A variety of bookmarks have made an appearance in works of literature. Louse in Graham Greene's *The Heart of the Matter* was said to be an avid reader who used *"hairpins, inside the library books where she had marked her place."* Christine, the professor in Tessa Hadley's short story, *Mother's Son*, used a widely employed bookmarking technique: *"…books by Rhys and Woolf and Bowen were piled all around her, some of them open face down on the table, some of them bristling with torn bits of papers as bookmarks."* More recently, and to my relief, the art of bookmarking has been restored to its aesthetic integrity by Michael Ondaatje in *Divisadero*: *"Once Lucien picked up a book that the thief had been reading and saw a sprig of absinthe leaves used as a bookmark. That felt like the only certain thing about the man, and from then on, every few days, the writer carefully noted the progress of the absinthe, making its own journey through the plot."*

The other day I asked my wife, a voracious reader, if she had thought much about the place of bookmarks in her reading life. She replied quite simply that she never uses a bookmark, with the clear implication that my question was pretty stupid. I thought that odd at the time, until I realized she usually reads a book from start to finish, so obviously she would have no need for anything as mundane as a bookmark. Neither did my aunt, who, I recalled the other day, used to tear each page out of a book once she had finished reading it. What a booklover she was! Of course, I only saw her do that when she was reading cheap paperback novels. Since I never saw her reading anything else, I doubt if she ever had need for anything as humdrum as a bookmark.

On the other hand, another reader friend of mine reports that she has a special fondness for bookmarks largely because she often makes her own. She recounted the construction of several such occasions when she was at the beach with her daughter and grandchildren. The bookmarks they made that day included glued shells, sand, and seagull feathers. It was a good memory for her. Another came fromwas a time when she was sitting around with some close friends and someone suggested they make bookmarks for one another. She still has a couple of those, and every time she uses one, it reminds her of some special people and the times they've were had together.

Recently I have recently adopted the practice of ordering some of my books on the Internet, almost exclusively from Amazon.com. I don't always like doing that because it comes at the expense of my favorite local bookshops. But Amazon is quick and convenient, and I don't have to suit up in the winter to go over to Powell's or Twenty-Third Avenue Books. Amazon almost always has a new copy of every book I want, and then some.

In the old days, Amazon used to send me an attractive bookmark along with each order. They were made of firm paper, colorfully decorated, were a goodly length (8 inches), and adorned with a booklover's quote on one side. *A book is like a garden carried in the pocket.* (Chinese Proverb). *When I get a little money I buy books; and if any is left I buy food and clothes* (Erasmus). *The test of literature is, I suppose, whether we ourselves live more intensely for the reading of it* (Elizabeth Drew). *When you sell a man a book, you don't sell him 12 ounces of paper and ink and glue—you sell him a whole new life* (Christopher Morley).

A few years ago, Amazon stopped including bookmarks with my order. That was unfortunate. I still have every one they sent me housed in my box of favorite bookmarks. I wonder why they stopped the practice? I must e-mail Jeff Bezos to find out. He has become one of my virtual friends, and I often send him an e-mail. But instead of attractive bookmarks, he now sends me a traveling coffee mug each Christmas. Quite frankly, I'd prefer a bookmark with an expression that reminds me how lucky I am to be able to read the books in the packages that he sends.

I have been going to Italy a great deal lately. I don't know exactly why, except that I have come to feel at home there and am rather taken with the life and beauty that surrounds me. Most of the time I stay in Florence, where I rent an apartment for a month or two. Over the years, I have discovered all the English language bookstores in the Centro, some of which rival anything you might find in this country or England. Each one has its own bookmark that has been duly added to my collection. But mostly I've been accumulating those with beautiful pictures of the Tuscan landscape. They are just the right size, printed on heavy paper, with a photograph in the center—a field of sunflowers, a villa in the distance, vines hanging limp with grapes, the golden hillsides of Tuscany.

Along with its countless works of art and historical monuments, Florence is also known as a center for printing fine paper. One of the most renowned printers is the Bottega d'Arte Guilio Ginnini & Figlio. They have designed a distinctive tri-fold bookmark that describes in four languages their fine paper products, including sheets of paper salvaged from the books that were irreparably damaged in the great Florentine flood of 1966. It is not surprising that this has become one of my most cherished bookmarks, also housed quite naturally in my special bookmark box.

Bookmarks have not escaped the wonders of the digital age either. A 21st century reader can now purchase a digital bookmark with a built-in dictionary, the ever-popular Selco Bookmark Dictionary II. It is said to hold 130,000 words with "definitions thoroughly revised and updated." They can be had at Amazon.com for a little over $35. Whoever heard of paying for a bookmark? The "keypad" of this gadget is no thicker than your ordinary bookmark. However, it is attached at the top to a modest-size LCD screen that not only displays the meaning of words, but when it is not in the dictionary mode, also the date and time of day for readers who can't live without this information. There is a scrolling feature for those wordy definitions, plus a key for viewing the previous definition. As if that is not enough, it also incorporates a calculator, for readers who are trying to solve Fermant's Last Theorem. I have been rendered speechless by the thing. The screen sits up upon the top of the keypad, like Humpty-Dumpty on his wall. I have a feeling it won't be long before my jazzy new Selco Bookmark Dictionary II will experience a similar fate.

For readers who are ready to upgrade to a four-star deluxe bookmark, I can report that Tiffany's new bamboo leaf/scarab bookmark in sterling silver is now available. I saw it advertised in *The Times* the other day and was duly informed that it is designed for bookmark lovers who want to add a touch of glamour to their favorite coffee-table book. Each one is carefully embossed with bamboo stalks and a tiny copper and gold beetle. At $120, it would make a perfect Christmas gift for all your bookish friends. You don't live near a Tiffany store? No problem, just go to www.tiffany.com to order this gem. Better do so before they run out; I am sure the supply is limited.

Recently the Internet has recently given birth to a new meaning for the word "bookmark." Now there are digital bookmarks to accompany all those "real world" versions that have given readers such pleasure over the centuries. If you asked someone today to describe a bookmark, they are likely to tell you it is one of their favorite Web pages that can be reached by clicking on its link in the browser they are using. Of course, there is nothing aesthetically appealing about these kinds of bookmarks, nor does their appearance vary in any particular respect. They are surely not going to be collected or treasured like the bookmarks of yesteryear, and no one is going to get very choosy about how they look or feel either.

It bothers me a bit to dilute the meaning of an object that is as richly valued as a bookmark that we use in reading a book. So I have been thinking it might really be a really good idea to think of another way to refer to the Web pages that we want to remember. How about webmark, virtualmark or digimark? Any of those terms would do. Don't they denote more accurately what a website is than does the word "bookmark"?

There is even a site on the Web now devoted exclusively to the topic of bookmarks. While not the most popular of sites, on the Web (since February 2001, it has had over 21,000 visitors), if you go to www.miragebookmark.ch/index.html, you will find links to a sizeable number of bookmark collections and exhibitions, documents on the history of bookmarks, and information about exchanging books with other collectors. You could also visit a site on how to make bookmarks, as well as a host of other web-shops to purchase them. In fact, recently I also did a bookmark search on www.ebay.com, and, to my amazement, discovered there were over twelve pages displaying more than 575 bookmark collections that you could bid on there. Who would have believed that the world of bookmarks is so vast?

The beautiful book of the bookmark exhibition in Milan set the occasion for my ramblings about this world; I'm still not quite sure why it did. But once I started, it was not difficult to keep going. And in doing so, I began to appreciate that bookmarks are not just for marking a page in the books I am reading. To be sure, I want them to do that but I also want them to do the job reliably; that is, I don't want them to fall out or bend easily or be so flimsy that they quickly begin to crumble.

Yes, it never hurts if they are also aesthetically pleasing or informative in some way, say by including a memorable passage about reading by a well-known writer, or a thoughtful review of the book I am reading. It is no less important that they be worth preserving for some reason. I don't collect a great many objects. I may save a few postcards from places I have been in my travels, or photographs of the special people in my life, or treasures that someone has made for me. But that's about it.... except, of course, for the bookmarks from my favorite bookstores.

Each of the treasured bookmarks in my little box conjures up a memory of the bookstore, the town where it is located, its size, the quality of its collection, the light in the store, and the feeling that comes to me when I am there. In this sense, a bookmark is indistinguishable from any memento, say a photograph or a trinket from a place I have been. Both seek to preserve an experience that was in some way memorable and don't want to forget. For my friend who makes bookmarks, it is the memories of some people who helped her construct them. For me it is primarily the memories of the good times I have had in the places where I found them. In this way, a bookmark does its part, albeit a small one, to sustain the culture of reading and all that follows from that experience. This is not to be taken lightly in an age when reading literature is said to be on the wane.

Science Writing: Revisiting Blink[50]

Someone who says "yes" too quickly is probably not as interesting as someone who replies more slowly.
Susan Orlean[51]

What are the special responsibilities of a science writer whose work is widely read and much admired? I have pondered this question for several years now, ever since I began reading the sometimes dazzling essays of Malcolm Gladwell. At first, I was deeply impressed by the way he wrote; several of his expressions and speculations have entered my Commonplace Book. He is a story-teller, a good one, and is able to bring alive the abstract findings of large and important areas of social science. His essays in *The New Yorker* are entertaining, instructive, and more often than not, concern issues of consequence.

But as time went by, I began to worry. As a social scientist with a good deal of applied research experience, I though Gladwell often simplified issues that were far more complicated than he acknowledged. I worried about the research he *didn't* talk about and the qualifications they placed upon his claims. I was troubled by his tendency to overgeneralize, as I knew the studies

50 I thank Penelope Stanton for the many contributions she has made to this essay.

51 Susan Orlean, *Wordstock Festival,* Portland, Oregon, April 24, 2005

he cited did not apply as widely as he implied. And then most of his essays consisted of a series of anecdotes or case studies with little in the way of analysis. A writer doesn't create a very deep understanding of human behavior from a cascade of entertaining anecdotes.

The very considerable popularity of his most recent book, *Blink: The Power of Thinking without Thinking*, first published in January 2005, has quickened my concern. At the time of this writing (July 2008) the paperback edition of *Blink* is ranked thirteen on *The New York Times* list of paperback nonfiction best sellers and 141 of the paperback books sold at Amazon.com. Both editions of *Blink* have been best sellers ever since they were published, as was true of Gladwell's equally popular *The Tipping Point*.

In *Blink*, Gladwell distinguishes between snap judgments and those made more deliberately. Snap judgments are made quickly, "in the blink of an eye," with little or no effort to think things over before responding, say by considering alternatives or seeking out additional information. On the other hand, deliberate judgments are made more slowly, after some thought is given to the issue-at-hand, usually by analyzing the situation or the implications of newly obtained information.

More than once Gladwell suggests that rapidly-made decisions are every bit as reliable as decisions made more cautiously. For example, in discussing the diagnosis of potential heart attack victims by emergency room physicians, he boldly concludes that "you need to know very little to find the underlying signature of complex phenomena." Or in discussing the initial impressions we form of other people when we meet them for the first time, he claims "…it is quite possible for people who have never met us and who have spent only twenty minutes thinking about us to come to a better understanding of who we are than people who have known us for years." (p. 36) Not even that much time is required during a speed-dating session, where he informs us we only need about six minutes of conversation. And students need even less, no more than two seconds, according to Gladwell, to judge how another group of students will rate a teacher's effectiveness after being in the class for a full semester.

Although Gladwell is not a professional psychologist, he is quite familiar with a wide spectrum of the discipline. However, he doesn't always get it right. As a case in point, consider his discussion of the study that he drew upon in describing our ability to extract very rapidly a feature of behavior or a situation based on a "thin slice" of behavior. The term is taken from the title of Nalini Ambady and Robert Rosenthal's report, *Half a Minute: Predicting Teacher Evaluations from Thin Slices of Nonverbal Behavior and Physical Attractiveness*.[52] Gladwell summarizes its findings as follows: "A person watching a silent two-second video clip of a teacher he or she has never met will reach conclusions about how good that teacher is that are very similar to those of a student who has sat in the class for an entire semester."

Well, that's not quite what Ambady and Rosenthal report. In

52 Nalini Ambady and Robert Rosenthal, Half a Minute: Predicting Teacher Evaluations from Thin Slices of Nonverbal Behavior and Physical Attractiveness. *Journal of Personality and Social Psychology*, 654, No. 3, 1993, 431-441.

fact, the "persons" who watched the video were actually a group of *female* undergraduates. Men were *excluded* from each of the three Ambady and Rosenthal studies on the basis of evidence that purports to show that women are better decoders of nonverbal behavior than men, a conclusion this author finds dubious at best, to say nothing of the limits an all-female sample imposes on the generality of the studies' findings.

In addition, the "two-second video clip" consisted of three two-second exposures for a total of six-seconds of viewing. A minor point to be sure, but a writer should get his facts straight. Again, the comparison in the more accurately called six-second video was not between two groups of students but rather between female undergraduates and the principal of the high school where the teachers shown on the video clip taught. Moreover, the female undergraduates did not actually rate the teacher's effectiveness after viewing the video. Instead, they were asked to rate the teacher on fifteen non-verbal behaviors, such as frown, smile, empathy, enthusiasm, etc.

Furthermore, the measure that was compared with the principal's judgment (the criterion measure) was a *composite* of the *average* female undergraduate ratings of the fifteen nonverbal behaviors. Thus, the female students never actually rated the teacher's *overall* teaching effectiveness, although Gladwell reports the findings as if they did, e.g. "how good that teacher is." In short, the findings were based on *aggregate* data derived from a sizable number of judgments about a set of non-verbal behaviors by a total of forty-eight female undergraduate raters.

Gladwell tells us nothing about the predictive value of any of the nonverbal dimensions or how the women varied in their overall appraisal of the teacher, whether, for example, some were better than others in this respect or, indeed, whether some might have preferred to wait until they had further information. We know that individuals vary widely in their ability to accurately judge other individuals and in their disposition to act on the basis of their immediate reactions. Gladwell says nothing about these important aspects of either the Ambady and Rosenthal study or any of the other investigations that he draws upon in *Blink*.

There is also the matter of what constitutes teaching effectiveness. The female undergraduates were asked to judge a set of teacher nonverbal behaviors. In Study 1 one where three 30-second video clips were shown, the end-of-semester student ratings were used. In Study 2 (three 30-second video clips) and Study 3 (three 5-second and three 2-second video clips) the criterion measure was the principal's rating of the teacher's effectiveness. Is that what we mean by teaching effectiveness, namely ratings given by students and administrators?

It is widely recognized that judging teaching effectiveness is fraught with difficulties. At the very least, multiple criteria should be used, including student performance in the course while it is being taught, as well as over the long term after they have had an opportunity to absorb fully the course materials and explore its subject matter in other areas. The courses you hated sometimes become those you value most. The teachers that bored you to death sometimes become your most appreciated.

In summary, I believe Gladwell's cursory treatment of Ambady and Rosenthal's study is not accurate. The reader is presented with a less than complete description of their findings and is scarcely in a position to think critically about his presentation without tracking down the original study in the journal where it was published, a task that no reader can be expected to undertake. Is it not Gladwell's responsibility as a science writer to provide a full and accurate account of the study including whatever information the reader might require to consider alternative accounts of the findings or, at least, a set of questions that one might normally raise in thinking about its surprising results? As it is, we are simply given a small "slice" of the study without critical analysis, one that is neatly consistent with Gladwell's argument. And so it is with most of the other studies that he draws upon in *Blink*.

Surely all of us who have been students recognize the folly of acting upon such a "thin slice" of classroom experience. Recently I enrolled in a non-fiction writing class taught by a well-known essayist, a writer who had long ago introduced me to the craft of personal essay writing. The instructor spent almost all of the first class by reading from one of his recent essays. I was appalled. He made no opening statement, presented no plan of study, did not lay out the goals of the course, nothing like that. He read another long essay the next day, but by then I was getting used to his routine. He seemed strangely distant, generally unsmiling, and offered very little in the way of chit-chat or friendly banter.

My first impression of his teaching effectiveness was dismal. I thought about dropping the class. But I had traveled some distance to enroll in the class. So I decided to stick it out, in spite of my initial impression. I'm glad I hung in there. The instructor warmed up as the days went by, so that at the end of the two week session he was no longer the dour, humorless person he was at the outset but the delightful, jesting, free associating one he is on the page. He likes to ramble. At the beginning of the last class (nothing was prepared for that either!) I asked him what he meant by "research?" He took off on a flight that lasted well over an hour, roaming all over the place and back again. It was fun. All of us in the class enjoyed it. So did he. So much for relying on thin slices of teaching effectiveness.

The major problem with Gladwell's catalogue of the triumphs of snap judgments is the limited treatment he gives to their trustworthiness. Surely a reader must wonder when to trust a snap judgment and when not to. Gladwell gives this question surprisingly little attention. He admits it is important to understand those situations where snap judgments can lead us astray. But he makes no attempt to examine at any length this matter or how one might go about developing guidelines for deciding when to trust them and when to suspend judgment until further information can be obtained.

Not surprisingly he treats this central issue by presenting a stream of colorful examples. He points to the so-called Warren Harding Effect, the danger of coming to a conclusion about a person on the basis of their appearance. "Many people who looked at Warren Harding saw how extraordinarily handsome and distinguished-looking he was and jumped to the immediate—and entirely unwarranted—conclusion that he was a man of courage and intelligence and integrity." After urging caution in relying too much on a person's appearance, he does not return to the potential pitfalls of snap judgments until the last chapter where he discusses, at some length, the consequences of the snap judgments police officers made when they encountered Amadou Diallo one night on a street in the Bronx.

There is really nothing inherently wrong in describing particular instances to support a more general point of view. Everyone recognizes they have sometimes erred in acting too quickly on the basis of a hastily arrived at decision. What distinguishes those decisions from those that are more reliable? *Blink* would have been a better book if Gladwell had considered this issue with more depth and analytic detail than he did. Such a presentation might have helped the reader to determine when they can have confidence in their snap judgments and when they should be viewed with some degree of caution. Gladwell would have no difficulty making comprehensible in a thoroughly engaging fashion recent research that would contribute to their understanding. The readers of *Blink* are at a disadvantage because he did not.

To be sure, Gladwell does point out that snap judgments are often based on prior experience and that their accuracy can be improved with training. Indeed, one of the goals he stated early in *Blink* was to convince readers that snap judgments can be "educated and controlled." Still, he speaks of John Gottman's research on predicting marital happiness after observing an hour of a couples' interaction or a decision-making algorithm for predicting cardiac arrest as if they were examples of snap judgments based on thin slices of evidence. In fact, both were developed after long and complicated testing procedures that involved sifting through a good deal of data and reviews of other studies, as well as many hours of personal experience. This is hardly a very speedy process.

In fact, it is hard to imagine many decisions that occur without prior experience or knowledge, even those that occur in the "blink of an eye." All of the examples he provides from the judgments made about the Kuoros statue to the Warren Harding effect, or the first impressions we form of other people, depend on prior knowledge even if we are not aware of the information at the time we respond. And when the judgment process fails, as it often does, it is usually because we lack the relevant information or have been poorly trained, as in the case of the rookie cops who mistook a wallet for a gun. The surest way to improve the accuracy of our "snap judgments" is to take the time to gather the relevant information or obtain the necessary training to guide us the next time we are faced with a similar situation.

Gladwell insists there are many situations where "haste does not make waste, when our snap judgments and first impressions offer a much better means of making sense of the world."[53] Is there not more convincing evidence about this important matter other than catalogue of tales, well told though they are? For example, one might compare a decision to purchase a car based

53 Interview on Malcolm Gladwell's website http://www.gladwell.com/blink

on a buyer's initial reaction with the one they make after thinking about it for a day or two, after they have gathered some information. Was the reaction they arrived at initially a reliable predictor of how they felt after waiting a bit? And did it vary as a function of the amount of information they were able to obtain? We all know from experience that we sometimes regret purchasing a product on the spur of the moment. These types of experiences remind us of the limits of precipitous judgments and how in the light of subsequent events or information they can turn out to have been in error.

What are readers going to think after reading Gladwell's case for the power of snap judgments? Will they be led to abandon the time consuming process of reasoning, of putting their decisions on hold for a moment while they gather a little information? Or will they conclude they might as well decide on the basis of their initial reaction? Why bother to carefully consider a decision when Gladwell informs us that "knowing less is knowing more?"

The real danger that I see in *Blink: The Power of Thinking Without Thinking* is Gladwell's apparent argument against the importance of serious inquiry in our daily decision-making process. At least, that is the conclusion I believe most readers will come to after reading the book. Urging greater reliance on "fast and frugal" decision making has the potential to undermine the value of gathering information, weighing the consequences, doing a little studying and thinking before reaching a decision. None of this is necessary when you believe "decisions made very quickly can be every bit as good as decisions made cautiously and deliberately." It is a matter of emphasis and the emphasis in *Blink* is clearly on the side of deciding rapidly on the basis of how you feel at the moment.

The continuing widespread popularity of *Blink* makes me all the more concerned about its impact. I believe its readers deserve a more balanced view, a more critical approach to the important domain it highlights. One narrative after another about decisions made in a flash is not very satisfying. When research is mentioned, it is assumed to be true without qualification as Gladwell moves on to another story. This reader would wish for larger view, a testable theory or hypothesis if you will, even if it can only be sketched at this time, to make sense of the large assortment of such tales, many of them quite interesting to be sure, although less and less so as yet another one unfolds.

It isn't necessary to write a technical article to present recent scientific findings in an entertaining and accurate way to the general public. What is most needed is a presentation that is at the same time accurate, analytic and readable. Gladwell can do this as well as any other science writer I know. He has done so brilliantly in some of his essays in the *New Yorker*, but not in *Blink*.

The costs of relying too much on rapid decision- making should be clear. As Gladwell points out in the describing the Daillo case, snap judgments can sometimes be disastrous, as well as irreversible—all the more reason to be extremely cautious in overemphasizing their benefits. Early in the book (p. 15)

Gladwell asks: "So, when should we trust our instincts, and when should we be wary of them? Answering that question is the second task of *Blink*." He never does. At least I am at a loss to even begin to answer the question either in the light of anything he says or on the basis of the current research on the matter. We have just begun to explore the conditions under which intuitive judgments can be trusted. Thus it is surely premature at this time to make broad generalizations about their superiority to a more deliberative reasoning process. Knowing when to trust snap judgments and when not to is not a matter that can be decided in the blink of an eye.

Annotating Ian McEwan's Saturday

The key word for the commonplace book is "annotated." It is not just an anthology; the compiler reacts to the passages he has chosen or tells what the passages have led him to think about. A piece of prose, a poem, an aphorism can trigger the mind to consider a parallel, to dredge something from the memory, or perhaps to speculate with further range and depth on the same theme.[54]

I marked forty-five separate passages in Ian McEwan's *Saturday*, an intellectually rich novel about a single day in the life of Henry Perowne, a British neurosurgeon. As is my practice and that of most other readers who keep a commonplace book, I did not annotate those selections at the time they were recorded. However, I paused to give some thought to many of them and have expanded upon those considerations in the following commentary.

Perowne is a deeply reflective man. He muses, ruminates, broods and wonders about one thing or another—the nature of his disciple, his family, the routine chores that occupy his day, and

---

54 William Cole. Speaking of Commonplace Books. *New York Times* May, 3, 1970.

the troublesome times in which he lives during the early years of the 21st century. The changing conditions of the contemporary world are a constant worry, as is the apparent decline of Western values and ideals. McEwan describes "the drift, the white noise of [Perowne's] solitary thought" and at one point characterizes his state as a "folly of overinterpretation."

In turn, I was led to ponder his musings and the extent to which I agreed with them or not. As a result, although it was not a very lengthy novel, it took me forever to read—a pleasure devoutly treasured by this reader. McEwan speculates a good deal about the origins of human behavior and difficulties of identifying them with any precision. Since I have been concerned with those very same issues throughout my professional life, I marked a goodly number where McEwan writes about this issue.

Parental Influence

It's a commonplace of parenting and modern genetics that parents have little or no influence on the characters of their children. You never know who you are going to get. Opportunities, health, prospects, accent, table manners—these might lie within your power to shape.

I have come to believe that the influence of parents on their children is more subtle than McEwan implies here. To be sure, you can never predict the outcome of your children's early experiences or their genetic heritage. But that, in itself, is not grounds for concluding parents have little influence on their children.

We hear much doubt expressed today about the direct impact of parents on their children's personality and adult behavior, indeed, whether or not they matter at all or matter as much as their peers. It is said, for example, that parental influence on their children has been overestimated. Studies of identical twins (reared apart or together) are cited to show that genetic factors control about a half of a person's intellect and personality. Other studies of fatherless children are said to be consistent with this evidence. Rearing a child without an adult male in the household appears to have very little *particular* impact on children. Instead, factors associated with income, frequency of moving, and peer relationships are said to matter more.

My own feeling is that these claims say less about the influence of parents on their children and far more about the methods used to obtain the evidence, especially the methods used to assess adult behavior and personality. Frankly, I do not believe these methods tap the important dimensions of human personality and intellectual ability. Nor do I think the findings have a very high degree of generality.

I also believe whatever influence parents have on their children is not likely to be very specific. Instead, their influence has much more to do with personality and character dimensions rather than specific behaviors, table manners included. We learn from our parents *very general aspects of character and motivation.* We learn to value learning, not any particular discipline. We see what it means to be generous and helpful, not any particular instance of these acts. In short, our parents provide exemplars for those deeper aspects of human character and feeling that are expressed in the sort of person we become.

Genetic Control

But what really determines the sort of person who's coming to live with you is which sperm finds which egg, how the cards in the two packs are chosen, then how they are shuffled, halved and spliced at the moment of recombination. Cheerful or neurotic, kind or greedy, curious or dull, expansive or shy and anywhere in between; it can be quite an affront to parental self-regard, just how much of the work has already been done.

No one can deny the powerful impact of genetic factors on personality and behavior, although the fine details of how this occurs remain a mystery. Still, to say that genes are "what really determines the sort of person who's coming to live with you" goes well beyond the evidence. It is a truism to say they interact and work in combination with environmental factors.

The real advances in our knowledge will come from determining the mechanism whereby genes exert their control and whether or not this mechanism is modifiable or reversible. We cannot change a person's eye color but we may be able to alter other characteristics that are under genetic control, such as height, weight and the risk of certain diseases. In such cases, well known diet, exercise, and general lifestyle patterns can be decisive.

I recall an early experiment in behavior genetics. Two strains of rats can be bred over successive generations that differ markedly in their aggressiveness, with one strain highly aggressive in the presence of another rat and the other very non-aggressive in the same situation. However, these differences can be completely reversed by varying their early rearing experiences.

When an aggressive strain is reared in the presence of other rats, they no longer attack other rats in adulthood. However, if this strain is raised in isolation, they continue to behave aggressively as adults. On the other hand, when the non-aggressive strain is raised in isolation, they become extremely aggressive as adults in the presence of other rats. But they do not behave this way if they are reared in a social situation.

In a word, some forms of behavior normally thought to be under genetic control can be modified and completely reversed under appropriate environmental conditions. This finding is not restricted to aggressive behavior or to rats. The principle has been demonstrated to hold with other behaviors and other species, including humans. There is, indeed, far more to determining "what really determines the sort of person" your child will be than the random meeting of two eggs.

Neurophysiological Effects

McEwan is clearly interested in many other current issues confronting the study of human behavior. Indeed, there are several long sections in *Saturday* that treat in highly technical and at times, chilling language various neurophysiological diseases and the surgical procedures that Perowne employs in attempting to restore normal brain function. I did not make note of any of these passages, largely because they were well beyond my comprehension. But were I a neuroscientist I might have. However I did note one passage concerning chemical factors governing the transmission of nerve impulses.

Who could ever reckon up the damage done to love and friendship and all hopes of happiness by a surfeit or depletion of this or that neurotransmitter?

For years I have pondered the mystery of my father's illness, the alternating cycles of depression and elation that governed his life. I wondered whatever was at work to give rise to this strange and sad mix of horrible and wonderful days. And I have read the countless accounts of the relationship between brain chemistry and this malady and the way it can sometimes be corrected by drugs that counteract whatever neurotransmitter malfunction exists to give an individual some relief, sometimes total relief, from its symptoms.

But all this has never really helped me to better understand his torments. Neither psychoanalytic therapy, the drugs available at that time, electroshock treatment, or the best private "rest homes," gave him any lasting relief. Would the newer drugs and treatments available today have made a difference? Perhaps they might have made it easier for him to manage the furies more effectively or put them at a greater distance.

However, I am not at all sure about this and I remain a skeptic about the current views of the brain mechanisms that may be responsible for what is now known as bi-polar disorder. Yes, he may have had some kind of chemical imbalance, but I saw the world in which he grew up, the way his mother and father treated him, and how he had to spend his working days in the family business. It was never a placid situation. There was no escaping the world he brought with him but neither could he escape the one he had to live through during each and every day of his relatively brief life.

Non-Verbal Behavior

In several sections of *Saturday* Perowne mulls over the significance of the odd quirks of his patients and those he encounters during the course of that day. For example, the moment he sees Baxter, the driver of the car he bumped into, Perowne senses something about him is not quite right. He notes at once signs of "poor self control, emotional lability, explosive temper suggestive of reduced levels of GABA among the appropriate binding sites on striatal neurons." Perowne is truly a diagnostician of the first order. I made note of other passages in which McEwan ponders the meaning of non-verbal behaviors, including the following one:

> But can anyone really know the sign, the tell of an honest man? There's been some good work on this very question. Perowne has read Paul Ekman on the subject. In the smile of a self-conscious liar certain muscle groups in the face are not activated. They only come to life as the expression of genuine feeling. The smile of a deceiver is flawed, insufficient.

It seems that at almost every moment of waking life, we attempt to make inferences about other individuals based on incomplete knowledge or unreliable indicators. Often I wonder what can you tell about a person by the e-mails they write? Are they telling the truth or performing before you in this communicating medium? Do their words reflect authentic self, the one you would encounter when you meet them?

Here I think the issue is not so much the authenticity of the e-mailer but rather the accuracy of the attribution process. How often I have been struck by the discrepancy between the picture I have of an e-mail correspondent whom I have yet to meet and the reality of the person once we do eventually come face to face.

A person once told me she was charmed by the words in my e-mails but that the real me was not the least bit appealing. And in an essay on an online relationship she had formed, Megham Daum writes *"...though we both knew that the "me" in his mind consisted largely of himself... I was horrified by the realization that I had invested so heavily in a made-up character ..."* She was somewhat taken aback when she finally met the person she had been e-mailing for months and notes that if she had met him at a party she would have scarcely spoken to him.

To the best of my knowledge no one has investigated the accuracy of perceptions formed from e-mail messages. I find the issue fascinating and because it is so commonplace now, I am sure it will be examined before too long. Here the question is really no different than determining the truth of what another person says on the basis of their facial expression or the way they express themselves in ordinary language as conveyed by the words they write on their keyboard. People vary widely in the style and manner they write e-mails and this must surely be related to other aspects of their personality and character.

Scientific Truth

In *Saturday* and elsewhere McEwan has expressed his optimism about the ability of science to unravel the mysteries of the brain and the truth about consciousness. There are several passages in *Saturday* that deal with general matters of scientific inquiry and method. I was especially struck by this succinct remark.

...statistical probabilities are not the same as truths.

This claim is at the heart of the disenchantment I began to experience with the work I was doing in psychology. Psychologists seek to establish very general laws of human thought and action. Yet I never understood how evidence derived by averaging the scores of a group of individuals could serve as the foundation for a science of *individual* behavior. Laws based on such aggregate data tell us very little about specific individuals and serve only to obscure crucial features of human variability and uniqueness. Further, the many exceptions to these laws severely limit their generality. Thus, it is impossible to say with much confidence that they hold for a particular individual at a particular time and place.

This conclusion is not unlike one often voiced in judicial proceedings, where the legal standing of psychological research is also called into question. It took me a while to understand why courts were so hesitant to admit social science evidence, let alone take it seriously in adjudicating cases. Yet legal cases are decided on an *individual* basis and so, even when the weight of evidence clearly supports the relevant social science generalization, the courts still require "proof" that it applies in the case being adjudicated. When judges ask psychologists to link the general principle to the specific case, it is difficult, if not impossible for them to do so with certainty. But that is what the law requires. Psychologists can provide relevant case knowledge and guidance, but the information they present is rarely, if ever, decisive in judicial decision-making.

Similarly, I know enough about psychology to be wary of psychological generalizations and the statistical methods brought to the data they obtain. You can never be entirely confident about the applicability of evidence derived from this approach. I have come to believe that psychology will always have to be content with this sort of limitation. Laws based on group means hold for some people, some of the time, but one never can be sure on any given occasion if they apply to a particular individual in the situation at hand.

Fortuitous Events

Random events play a key role in many of the situations described in *Saturday*. The random combination of two embryonic eggs is said to determine a great deal about a person. The collision of the cars driven by Perowne and Baxter was a largely fortuitous event that might not have happened had either driver taken a different route or varied the speed they were driving. Elsewhere McEwan highlights the role of chance encounters in human events.

> *It troubles him to consider the powerful currents and fine turning that alter fates, the close and distant influences, the accidents of character and circumstance…*

> *The random ordering of the world, the unimaginable odds against any particular condition, still please him.*

Most accounts of personal change have neglected the powerful role of such events. One need only reflect on the major changes in their own life to realize the significance they have. When I ask students how their parents met, many report it was due to a chance meeting. One reported that his father was driving home from a business meeting and was involved in a serious automobile accident that required several weeks of hospital recuperation. The student's mother was his father's nurse and six months later they were married.

In a *New Yorker* profile, the late Yitzhak Rabin, former Prime Minister of Israel, described how he met his wife: "It began with a chance encounter in a Tel Aviv street in 1944; a glance, a word, a stirring within and then a further meeting." Nancy Reagan, wife of the former President Ronald Reagan, experienced a similar turn of events. In response to her concern over the receipt of a series of mail announcements of Communist party meetings that were intended for another person with the same name, she sought the advice of Ronald Reagan, then president of the Screen Actors Guild. Not long after that they were married.

A chance encounter between two individuals is not a totally random event. Rather it is the intersection of their lawfully governed paths, like the embryonic eggs or the two automobiles, that occurs by chance and can sometimes launch two individuals together on an entirely new one. Had the chance encounter not occurred, the two lives might have taken an entirely different course.

Social Change

No more big ideas. The world must improve, if at all, by tiny steps. People mostly take an existential view— having to sweep the streets for a living looks like simple bad luck. It's not a visionary age. The streets need to be cleaned.

People often wonder why they should bother to vote when their vote doesn't matter anyway. Or they ask why should they go to the trouble of taking the bus, when their attempt to save energy or reduce pollution in these ways isn't going to have the slightest effect on either of these problems.

Those who argue like this ignore a fundamental principle of social change. Although any single act has only a very modest effect, the cumulative impact of each individual act can be quite substantial. For example, relatively modest energy savings at the individual level, say by turning down your thermostat or taking the bus once a week, can lead to rather considerable energy savings when projected at the aggregate level.

The same is true for any situation that is influenced by the collective action of a large number of individuals. No one member of the population can determine the outcome of an election, but a large group of like-minded voters can. One need only recall recent elections in which candidates were victorious by margins of only one or two votes. If you voted for the winning candidate in this kind situation, it is clear that your vote made a difference. If you didn't vote for the losing candidate, again it is clear that your vote mattered. When taken together the individual actions of a small number of individual voters can have a very powerful effect on election outcomes.

Individuals have to believe that what they do matters even though it is often difficult for them to appreciate this in any real sense. Isn't one of the major issues then one of counteracting this widespread belief? Describing the Tragedy of the Commons might be one way. Imagine a group of herdsmen grazing their cattle on a common range. To increase their profits, each is motivated to add a new animal to their herd. Since a herdsman will initially profit by doing so, each adds further animals to his herd. As a result, there is an inevitable increase in the total number of animals. This leads very quickly to a serious overgrazing problem. The range is simply not adequate to support the increasing number of animals and, as its resources are gradually depleted, the animals in turn, are unable to survive. This eventually ends with the tragic ruin of all the herdsman.

It was Garrett Hardin who originally has described such a situation as the "Tragedy of Commons " arguing that the logic of the commons operates whenever individuals have unlimited access to a cheap but finite resource. This logic dictates that through the rational actions of individuals pursuing their own well-being, the resources will inevitably be exploited until they can no longer support the population at large. Similarly John Platt has characterized such situations as "social traps." He suggests that such traps occur when individuals, by pursuing their own self-interests, produce consequences that collectively are damaging to the group as a whole.

These concepts capture rather vividly the way in which the individual actions of a small group of individuals can influence a much larger population and the community as a whole. At the same time, they suggest how this logic can also be applied to the preservation of these resources. When the separate actions of individuals, say by driving less or using alternative transportation, are multiplied countless times over, year after year across a large number of individuals, their collective impact can be enormous.

In short, by thinking twice about their short term interests, individuals can not only benefit the community as a whole but themselves as well. There is nothing glamorous about these actions or the least bit visionary, but little by little, with these "tiny steps" they will keep the air clearer and the gas flowing at the pumps.

Literary Experience

There is some discussion of literature in *Saturday*, as Perowne's daughter is a poet and he is amused by her tutorials to try to get him up to speed about literary works. They have some delightful exchanges about his lack of interest in following her lead. And it is clear that Perowne is not much of a reader. So even though he is a deeply reflective man, I suppose one should not have been surprised, as I was at first, by the following passage.

> *Henry read the whole of Anna Karenia and Madame Bovary, two acknowledged masterpieces. At the cost of slowing his mental processes and many hours of his valuable time, he committed himself to the shifting intricacies of these sophisticated fairy stories. What did he grasp after all? That adultery is understandable but wrong, that nineteeth-century women had a hard time of it, that Moscow and the Russian countryside and provincial France were once just so.*

Yet it was literature that saved the lives of Henry Perowne and his family in *Saturday*. It occurred in a dramatic incident when Perowne returns home after a harrowing day about the time the United States was about to launch its second war in Iraq. On the way to his early morning squash match, Perowne has a minor automobile collision with a person he senses at once is a criminal with an irreversible brain disease.

Later that day, the criminal returns to Perowne's home to take revenge on him and those in his family, who have gathered to welcome the return of Daisy. Baxter, the criminal, is holding a knife to Perowne's wife, Rosalind, and asks Daisy, whom he has told to strip, to read from her newly published book of poems. She is terrified, doesn't know if she can begin or what to read, and looks to her poet grandfather, Grammaticus, for a hint. He senses her dilemma and tells her to read the one she used to recite for him. Daisy catches the hint at once and begins reciting *Dover Beach*.

Baxter is transfixed by the beauty of the poem. "You wrote that. You wrote that," he says in amazement. He asks her to read it again. When she is done reciting, Baxter's mood changes suddenly. He is thoroughly disarmed, overcome, as McEwan writes, by "a yearning he could barely begin to define." He removes the knife from Rosalind's neck, puts it back in his pocket, and tells his sidekick he has changed his mind. The tension is broken, the threat is over, and the overpowering of Baxter can begin.

Here, in the extreme, is the power of literature.

> *Daisy recited a poem that cast a spell on one man. Perhaps any poem would have done the trick, and thrown the switch on a sudden mood change. Still, Baxter fell for the magic, he was transfixed by it, and he was reminded how much he wanted to live.*

The experience is not only the stuff of fiction. While not exactly a work of literature, reading from a book called *The Purpose-Driven Life* played a central role in saving the life of Ashley Smith, who was recently held hostage for hours in her suburban apartment near Atlanta by Brian Nicholas, on the run after killing two people during his escape from a courthouse trial for an earlier murder. Smith claims that reading and speaking with

Nicholas about the book gave her a chance to simply talk with him and begin the process of gaining his trust so that he would allow her to leave her apartment so that she could see her daughter. Once out of the apartment, Smith called 911; Nicholas was captured moments later. Who knows what might have happened had she not been able to read sections of the book to Nicholas?

An Inquiring Mind

Gregorius did what he had always done when he was
unsure: He opened up a book.
Pascal Mercier

What can we learn about individuals from the books they write
or the reports of their friends, family members or lovers? Do
we get a glimpse of people as we might find them if we knew
them first-hand and as they might convey in describing their
thoughts or feelings? I am confronted by this question as I try
to tell you about two individuals — Amadeu de Prado and
Raimund Gregorious, and why I admired them so much. I never
met either of these men, nor did anyone else as far as I can tell.
Rather they are the fictional creations of a Swiss novelist and
philosopher writing under the name of Pascal Mercier in his
recently published novel, *Night Train to Lisbon*. This makes the
task of drawing a portrait of Prado and Gregorious even more
difficult, also more fun.

There is really very little plot to the novel. Indeed, one reviewer
noted it is largely talk—talk, talk, talk. That is true but even
more it is mostly questions—questions, questions, questions.
That is precisely why I liked the novel so much and why I liked
the individuals who raised all these questions in the first place.

The questions either posed issues I have given a good deal of thought to and have been thinking about a good deal of my life, or they posed new ones that drew me to ones that I felt deserved to be considered. It is a rare treat to read a novel about such individuals and an even greater one to carry on a conversation with them as I sometimes do when I talk to the fictional characters in the books I read.

Night Train to Lisbon begins by describing a typical day in the life of Raimund Gregorious, a day that is as fixed and orderly as any other day in his life—at least in the beginning. Gregorious is a classics professor and linguistic scholar living in Bern, Switzerland with a working knowledge of at least a half dozen languages and a vast knowledge of ancient history and texts. Following a bizarre series of events on what otherwise would have been his daily walk to work, Gregorious comes in possession of volume written by a Portuguese physician, Amadeu de Prado. He is overtaken by the volume's eloquence and intellectual brilliance and is so consumed by its contents that, in striking departure from his daily routine, he leaves his class in mid-session and sets off for Portugal to learn more about the author and the sources of his extraordinary document.

He learns that Prado was a highly respected doctor, a brilliant scholar and a member of the resistance movement in opposition to the Portuguese dictator Antonio Salazar. Gregorious asks: "Was it possible that the best way to make sure of yourself was to know and understand someone else?" Perhaps because of his growing sense that his own time was running out, as well as his curiosity about Prado, Gregorious comes to realize that he would like to know everything he can about him. This quest brings him into contact with Prado's two sisters, a close friend, and two women, the "untouched" loves of his life.

While Gregorious's spur-of-the-moment breakout quest to Lisbon and encounters with these individuals is not without its appeal, it was not the major reason I found *Night Train to Lisbon* every bit as fascinating as Gregorious found the Portuguese volume. Rather it was the questions Amadeu de Prado raised in his volume, *A Goldsmith of Words*, and in turn considered by Gregorious as he read the text and brooded over its rich and varied meanings. As is my practice, I recorded the passages in the novel that struck me as noteworthy for one reason or another. And when I reviewed those I had collected, I realized how many were framed as questions, often one after another in a cascade of queries.

Consider the following examples concerned with one of the central issues of the novel—how one comes to know another person, including oneself.

> *How can you tell whether to take a feeling seriously or treat it as a carefree mood?*

> *The stories others tell about you and the stories you tell about yourself: which come closer to the truth?*

> *In such stories, is there really a difference between true and false?*

*What do we know of somebody if we know nothing
of the images passed to him by his imagination?*

*To understand yourself: Is that a discovery or a
creation?*

What difficult questions. Who has not wondered about them at
one time or another? How complicated and unknowable we are.
How then can we ever expect to know another person? Mercier
writes:

*We are in the dark about so many of our wishes and
thoughts, and others sometimes know more about
them than we do.*

And, as if to take issue with current empirical research on
person perception, he proclaims:

*Inside a person it is much more complicated than our
schematic, ridiculous explanations wanted to have us
believe.*

In a similar vein, Mercier, by way of Prado, wonders a great deal
about the problem of identity. Who are we anyway? Are we the
same person today that we were 40 years ago? If so, what is it
that constitutes our core, or does that concept mean anything at
all? Prado inquires:

*When was somebody himself? When he was as always?
As he saw himself? Or as he was when the white hot*

lava of thoughts and feelings buried all lies, masks, and self-deceptions?

Is there a mystery under the surfaces of human action? Or are human beings utterly what their obvious acts indicate?

Does it make any sense to say that a person has a central self, a distinctive identity that lies hidden behind most of the actions that constitute daily life? I sometimes find myself in the presence of another person who, for entirely unknown reasons calls forth expressions that somehow seem far more myself than is usually the case. How does that happen? Who is the me that appears in such situations and how does it differ from my other self or selves? Nothing that I have been able to detect in the other person seems responsible. But what I am on those rare occasions is instantaneous and continuous and thoroughly exhilarating. It seems entirely natural and I have no idea what to make of it.

Gregorious had devoted his life to linguistic scholarship, so he was naturally drawn to Prado's frequent speculations about language and amazement *"That words could cause something in the world, make someone move or stop, laugh or cry..."* Elsewhere he asks:

Saying something to another: how can we expect it to affect anything? How could a person almost lose his mind because a word, a single word, that occurred one single time, had escaped him?

How does complicated, analytical thought related to intuitive certainty? Which of the two should we trust more?

These questions always remain unanswered. Neither Prado or Gregorious consider how one might go about trying to examine them or what others have said about these issues. The questions just keep unfolding, one after the other, each one as interesting as the one before. Many are the subjects of current research and writing in the cognitive sciences, the discussion of which is surely out of place in the novel, but on the mind of anyone vaguely familiar with this field. The extraordinary popularity of Malcolm Gladwell's recent book, *Blink: The Power of Thinking without Thinking* is a case in point, as it takes up the very same issue Prado poses in his question about the relative merits of analytical and intuitive decision-making. The same is true for other recent works on the extent to which irrational, non-conscious processes govern far more of the decision-making process than we usually believe.

Throughout his volume, Prado reflects on the sources of human thought and action. He knows how difficult it is to identify them with any precision, that they vary widely between individuals, and from one day to the next.

If it is the enchanting light of a shimmering August day that produces clear, sharp-edged shadows, the thought of a hidden human depth seems bizarre and like a curious, even slightly touching fantasy....

On the other hand, if city and river are clouded over on

a dreary January day by a dome of shadowless light
and boring gray, I know no greater certainty than this:
that all human action is only an extremely imperfect,
ridiculously helpless expression of a hidden internal
life of unimagined depths that presses to the surface
without ever being able to reach it even remotely.

At the time he wrote *A Goldsmith of Words*, Portugal was under the sway of the dictator, Alberto Salazar. After saving the life of the head of Salazar's secret police under conditions that depended more on his obligations as a physician than political allegiance, Prado joined the resistance. At this point his life became even more perilous than it was for any intellectual at that time. The subject of violent behavior, especially interpersonal violence is a constant theme of his volume.

What could it mean to deal appropriately with anger?

What can it mean to train ourselves in anger and imagine that we take advantage of its knowledge without being addicted to its poison?

Why did our parents, teachers and other instructors never talk to us about it? Why didn't they tell something of this enormous significance? Not give us in this case any compass that could have helped us avoid wasting our souls on useless, self-destructive anger?

For all his brilliance, enthusiasms, and honesty, Prado was a melancholy man who in most respects stood apart from others. He felt his isolation keenly, writing:

Encounters between people, it often seems to me, are like crossings of racing trains at breakneck speed in the deepest night. We cast fleeting, rushed looks at the others sitting behind dull glass in dim light, who disappear from our field of visions as soon as we barely have time to perceive them.

And he kept searching for someone who understood him, who could keep up with him, who was as alive and questioning as he was. He asked:

And why had he never had a friend as Jorge O'Kelly had been for Prado—A friend with whom he could have talked about things like loyalty and love, and about death?

What is it that we call loneliness, it can't simply be the absence of others, you can be alone and not lonely, and you can be among people and yet be lonely? So what is it?

Is it so that everything we do is done out of fear of loneliness? ......Why else do we hold on to all these broken marriages, false friendships, boring birthday parties? What would happen if we refused all that, put an end to the skulking blackmail and stood on our own?

Why hadn't there been anybody before in his life who understood him so fast and so easily?

In reading *Night Train to Lisbon* I was not deliberately looking for passages that posed questions. It was only after finishing the book that I began to look closely at those I had recorded and realized how many were framed this way. In fact, of the 120 passages I recorded from the book, a number that may be the most in my reading history, forty-seven (forty per cent) included at least one question. I began to wonder if questioning also played a similar role in the passages I recorded from other books that have meant a lot to me.

I copied forty-six passages from Ian McEwan's *Saturday*, a book I enjoyed every bit as much as *Night Train to Lisbon* but of these quotations, only seven (fifteen per cent) included a question. Similarly, I recorded forty-seven passages in Philip Roth's *Exit Ghost* and of these only seven (fifteen per cent) included a question. And of the eighty-three passages I recorded in Elliot Perlman's *Seven Types of Ambiguity*, just seven (eight per cent) included a question. In contrast, I recorded eighty-three passages in Rachel Cusk's *Arlington Park*, a book that entranced me for days, and of these twenty-eight (forty-one percent) included a question, a value that is approximately the same as Mercier's tale.

It is clear from this small sample that questioning is not a critical feature of the novels I like most. I may enjoy that style of writing and tend to think that way myself, but it probably plays little if any role in my reading preferences. Henry

Perowne, the central character in Ian McEwan's *Saturday* is depicted as a deeply reflective man who spends a good part of that day at least, wondering about a wide range of topics. But his reflections are rarely formulated as questions.

It would be interesting to compare writers on this dimension. Do some employ questioning more than others and if so, what might be responsible for their practice? Do they come from a particular tradition or are they, like Pascal Mercier, derived from his discipline (philosophy) where questioning is a central practice? Regardless, it reflects a style of writing that is one of probing and wrestling with ideas. Many of Prado's questions are posed for rhetorical effect rather than a direct answer. That is, the answer is simply implied by the question. Prado says: *We humans: what do we know of one another?* Clearly he implies that we know very little. Still he wants the reader to consider the issue and give some thought to the implications of the implied answer. It is a style of writing that encourages an internal dialogue for any reader who takes the text seriously. And it is a habit of mind I find very congenial.

In addition to a style of writing, I have noticed a similar manner in the way individuals converse with one another. Some ask a great many questions, while others might ask one or two and, more commonly, none at all. Perhaps questioning as a mode of conversation, indeed, as a way of thinking, is a distinct personality dimension. My hunch is that it is strongly associated with a philosophical turn of mind, a general skepticism about most beliefs and at least, a continuing effort to look more deeply into the claims of others whether they are expressed in conversation or the printed page. That is clearly true of Amadeu and Gregorious.

In contrast, other individuals seem more accepting of whatever it is they hear or read and tend to comment, if they say anything at all, with a "That is really interesting" or "It reminds me of this or that" or simply change the subject altogether. They are unlikely to express any doubts or seek clarification or evidence, especially contrary evidence, relevant to the matter at hand.

Those of the questioning frame of mind use an approach not unlike that of a Socratic dialogue, where conversation becomes a progression of questions designed to arrive at a conclusion beyond the originally stated position. Some people are quite comfortable with this kind of discussion. For them it becomes a truly joint exchange in the interest of clarifying thinking and sharpening beliefs and perhaps even learning something along the way. I sense those of the accepting frame of mind do not fall naturally into this mode of conversation and perhaps might find it difficult to sustain it for very long.

I recorded many other notable passages from *Night Train to Lisbon* that were not formulated as questions—sixty per cent, in fact. Some were simply beautiful, others took me by surprise, some rang true to my own experience, while still others were startlingly insightful. Here is a sampling of a few:

> *Encounters between people, it often seems to me, are*
> *like crossings of racing trains at breakneck speed in*

the deepest night. We cast fleeting, rushed looks at the others sitting behind dull glass in dim light, who disappear from our field of vision as soon as we barely have time to perceive them.

You saw his absence and encountered it as something tangible. His not being there was like the sharply outlined emptiness of a photo with a figure cut out precisely with scissors and now the missing figure is more important, more dominant than all the others.

An hour to Paris. Gregorius sat down in the dining car and looked out into a bright, early spring day. And there, all of a sudden, he realized that he was in fact making this trip—that it wasn't only a possibility, something he had thought up on a sleepless night and that could have been, but something that really and truly was taking place. And the more space he gave this feeling, the more it seemed to him that the relation of possibility and reality were beginning to change.

And so it went from one page to the next, from one set of questions to the next. A remarkable journey that began by abandoning an orderly life dedicated to classical languages for one in pursuit of an author he had never heard of, who had written a book in an unknown language, and lived in a city that he had never been to. He begins to translate the book, is captivated by its introspective musings, and one by one encounters the individuals Amadeu de Prado wrote about in *A Goldsmith of Words*. The tale is beautifully written and the questions it poses linger long in my mind, as does the reflective mood of the tale and its central characters.

In a word, some of my favorite novels have few if any questions, while others have a great many. They set me off in another direction for a moment, my mind wanders off the page, I elaborate the tale or move it to another place. I don't rewrite the story, but may embellish it a bit. I read more actively as I grapple with the questions or make all the associations that come with experience and a lifetime of study. In a way, I reply to the author who, with his questions, invites me to join with him telling the story. It is a reading experience at its best.

Does Literature Change Lives?

I don't believe that, in my society, novels affect serious changes in anyone other than the handful of people who are writers, whose own novels are of course seriously affected by other novelists' novels. I can't see anything like that happening to the ordinary reader, nor would I expect it to....You asked me if I thought my fiction had changed anything in the culture and the answer is no.
Philip Roth

I was changed by literature, not by cautionary or exhortatory literature, but by the truth as I found it in literature. I recognize the world in a different way because of it, and I continue to be influenced in that way by it. Opened up, made more alert, and called to a greater truthfulness in my own accounting of things, not just in my writing, in my life as well. It did that for me, and does that for me, and no one touched by it in this way should have any doubt of its necessity.
Tobias Wolff

Beyond my own reading experiences is the larger question of how other readers are affected by their literary encounters. The commonplace book tradition cannot thrive, let alone exist, in a culture where literary reading is on the wane. However, we hear from every quarter in this country that no one reads anymore, that television and now the Internet have all but killed off the pleasures of the page. We bemoan the closing of one bookstore after another and the alleged sharp decline in literary reading documented in the recent National Endowment for the Arts (NEA) report.[55] However, I am not entirely convinced by all these obituaries for reading, especially the widely cited NEA analysis. The study reports the findings of a large sample survey of over 17,000 individuals conducted by the Census Bureau in 2002. The survey was designed to learn more about public participation in the arts, including the extent of literary reading in this country.

To measure literary activity, individuals were asked to indicate whether or not they had read at least one literary work during the past year. A "literary work" was defined as a novel, short story, play, or work of poetry. A reported decline in literary reading of ten per cent (56% to 46.7%) from 1982 to 2002 was the finding that aroused the greatest concern. This trend was observed for all the demographic groups that were studied— gender, ethnicity, educational level, and age, with the steepest decline of twenty-eight per cent reported for those in the youngest age group, those between eighteen and twenty-four.

In my view, the study is flawed in several respects. The definition of literary work is unnecessarily narrow, as a person who has read a memoir, collection of essays, or historical biography is

55 *Reading at Risk: A Survey of Literary Reading in America*. National Endowment for the Arts, Research Division Report #476.

not counted as a literary reader. Similarly, a person who has read the novels of Tolstoy and Dostoyevsky in a Russian literature course is also excluded from this group. Moreover, the measurement procedure does not distinguish between various types of literary works—reading a book of Ogden Nash poems is considered equivalent to reading Tennyson, Proust, or Keats.

In truth, as documented in the report, a significant amount of reading occurs in this country, as almost sixty per cent of the US population indicated they have engaged in some form of literary activity during 2002. Moreover, given the rise in the population since 1982 (the year of the previous NEA survey), more people are reading literature today in terms of absolute numbers than in 1982, 205 million compared to 168 million, values that cannot be readily dismissed.

In a word, the implications of the NEA report may not be quite as dire as its authors imply. Perhaps individuals are reading more literary works on the Internet, or reading other literary genres, such as biography or political commentary or listening to literary works on tape, or simply spending more time reading periodicals and newspapers that on some accounts have the same benefits as the novels, short stories, plays, or works of poetry measured in the survey. Also, 2002 may not have been a representative year, as the profound effects of the attack on this nation in September of the preceding year were still very salient.[56]

Indeed, informal book clubs and reading groups are flourishing

---

56 Sampling yearly trends, rather than ten-year periods, would have provided a much clearer picture of the trends in literary activity.

throughout the country. Consider my hometown. Portland, Oregon is said to be a rather bookish city, with perhaps more bookstores per capita than any other comparable size city in the country. People seem to like to read, or at least to have books around for those long and dreary rainy days and nights. In a recent edition of *The Sunday Oregonian*, I was astonished to find that twenty-four different groups were scheduled to meet during the month and those were just the groups whose meetings were open to the public: The Great Books Group, The Popular Fiction Book Group, The Modern Women's Group, Contemporary Fiction, Science Fiction, and Gay, Lesbian, and Bisexual Book Groups, The Romance Readers Classic Books, First Wednesday, Mystery Lovers, Memoir, and Biography Groups, etc. etc. I was simply bowled over by the number of groups, the range of topics, and the fact that they were meeting regularly. Who would have imagined that so many people were doing so much reading?

Anecdotal Evidence

Recently I have begun to wonder how readers are influenced by experiences like this and by reading literature in general. Does a reader of literary works behave differently after their reading experiences than they would have otherwise? Or how are their beliefs or values changed by books they have read? The experience of reading a work of literature is rarely if ever, included among the influential agents of personal change. Yet many people report that it was a book that changed the course of their life or the lives of a large group of individuals. Goethe's *Sorrows of Young Werther* is perhaps the foremost example of the powerful impact of the reading experience. It led so many young individuals into acts of imitative suicide that it was banned in several countries soon after it was published.

Less dramatic effects have recently been reported on several sites on the Web. The San Francisco bookstore, A Clean Well-Lighted Place for Books, has a page on its website (*www.bookstore.com/bookschallenge.html*) that invites readers to "name the book that changed your life." One contributor responded: "The Harry Potter books changed my life. I used to hate reading. Now I am the best reader in the class. Those books changed my imagination. I wasn't too much of a dreamer. Now, I love to imagine things. I just hope that they change someone else's life like they did mine."

The Autodidactic Press also offers a similar invitation on the "Books that Changed Lives" page on its website (*www.autodidactic.com/changedlives.htm*). In citing *The Autobiography of Malcolm X*, one individual wrote: "I first read the book as a sixth grader. The book was so searing that I vowed to become like that unusual man. Today I am a Muslim as a direct result of Malcolm's autobiography."

The Academy of Achievement seeks to bring young students in this country into contact with the "greatest thinkers and achievers of the age." To encourage young individuals to develop a love of books, the Academy has created a website that has posted the responses of individuals it regards as "eminent achievers, to the question "What book did you read when you were young that most influenced your life?" (http://www.achievement.org/autodoc/books/1).

To date the Academy has recognized 142 achievers in five areas: the arts (46), business (14), public service (40), science (30) and sports (12). The website has posted detailed interviews with each of these individuals about their past and the keys to their success. Among the questions asked was one on notable books they had read in their youth: *"What book did you read when you were young that most influenced your life?"* The edited responses from individuals in three of the groups[57] are shown below:

Arts: Joyce Carol Oates

> *The one book, probably, of my young adolescence would have been Henry David Thoreau's Walden. That struck a very deep chord with me..... I think that I probably have grown up to have a Thoreauvian perspective on many things. He believed one should simplify, simplify, simplify.*

Business: Steve Case

> *One in particular that actually was a meaningful impact in terms of what I ended up doing — focusing on interactive service and the Internet — was a book I read in college in the late 1970s by Alvin Toffler called The Third Wave....This was 1979, and most people 25 years ago thought I was a little bit loony, but I just believed. And so I just kept pursuing that.*

Public Service: President James Carter

> *When people ask me what's a favorite book that I've*

---

57 Apparently the interviews with individuals in the field of sports did not include a question about their favorite book.

ever read, I used to say Let Us Now Praise Famous Men by James Agee ... who wrote about the lives of people who lived in desperate poverty.... What impressed me with that book was the tremendous chasm between people who have everything, who have a house and a job and education and adequate diets, and a sense of success or security ...and the vast array of people still in our country who don't have any of these things,.......and we are not doing much about it.

The way in which literature can shape a person's life has recently been the subject of three books.[58] In the first, *The Book That Changed My Life,* by Roxanne Coady and John Johannessen[59] 71 authors who gave a reading at the first author's bookstore were asked to write a short passage about a book that had a major effect on their life. In most cases, they wrote about a book that led them to become a writer. After reading the *Bluest Eye* by Toni Morrison, Dorothy Allison wrote: "If I could repay a tenth of what I owed this storyteller, this brave and wonderful woman on the page, I would give anything." And Frank Rich,

---

58 The issue has also been treated in Diane Osen (Ed) *The book that changed my life: Interviews with National Book Award Winners and Finalists.* 2002. Modern Library Paperback Edition. The title of this book is rather misleading as the subject matter of the interviews treats all manner of topics related to the lives of these writers. In only one or two cases does it deal explicitly with a book that changed a person's life. For example, David McCullough, a historian, describes the experience of reading *A Stillness of Appomattox* as if a "window had been thrown open." He says in retrospect, that he knows it changed his life.

59 Roxanne Coady & Joy Johannessen *The Book That Changed My Life: 71 Remarkable Writers Celebrate the Books that Matter Most to Them,* 2006. New York: Gotham Books.

former drama critic of the *New York Times*, wrote: "*Act One* [by Moss Hart] showed me a way out of my childhood. If Moss Hart could escape his circumstances through hard work, luck, the kindness of strangers, and the sheer force of his passion, maybe I could too."

Harriet Scott Chessman described a rarely mentioned book, Gertrude Stein's *Ida*. Chessman comments: "I loved this striking book for the courage it gave me to start looking for my own 'genius,' my own spirit, and my own writing life. Stein's influence was slow but profound." It is clear that many of the books mentioned by the writers have had a life-long influence on their life. Anita Diamant wrote: "Virginia Woolf's *A Room of One's Own* influenced me as a journalist and as a novelist in ways that continue to unfold."

The books selected by these writers constitute a mixture of literary fiction, poetry, drama, biography, history, memoir, and unlikely volumes such as the Sears Catalogue. Several writers mentioned books they had read as children—Nancy Drew Mysteries, *Charlotte's Web*, *A Child's Garden of Verse*, *The Little Engine That Could*. But literary fiction including both classical and contemporary novels, and in a few instances short story collections were the most commonly identified genre. Taken together, as Coady writes in the Introduction to the volume, these accounts are "a dramatic reminder that everywhere, every day, someone is changed, perhaps even saved, by words and stories."

A somewhat broader sample of individuals was drawn upon in

Canfield and Hendricks volume, *You've Got to Read This Book*.[60] This idea for this book emerged during a meeting of "transformation leaders, business consultants, and authors" who had gathered at the home of Jack Canfield to discuss ways to make the "world a better place." During a break, the topic of books came up and several members spoke of the books that had a major influence on their lives.

When the group reassembled, Gay Hendricks asked each person to describe a book that had changed their life. Hendricks notes, "What happened next was wonderful to behold." Each person spoke with an enthusiasm that "absolutely glowed." This experience led Canfield and Hendricks to conduct in-depth conversations" with fifty-five people about the books that had this sort of impact on their lives. In turn, the conversations were edited and reorganized by an associate into short essays about the way these books had shaped their lives.

It is not entirely clear how the fifty-five individuals whose edited accounts are presented in *You've Got to Read This Book!* were selected. They appear to be chosen because they had some acquaintance with the authors and in one way or another because they were "all doing valuable work in the world." They were from a variety of fields with the majority in the "self-help movement" including spiritual counselors, personal coaches, and motivational speakers. A large number came from the fields of marketing and technology and several were either writers or publishers.

60 Jack Canfield & Gay Hendricks. *You've Got to Read This Book: 55 People Tell the Story of the Book That Changed Their Life* 2006. New York: Harper Collins

It is also evident that a goodly number wore many hats, combining work in business and writing and personal training etc. For example, Pat Williams, the senior vice present of the NBA's Orlando Magic is described as "a motivational speaker, author of numerous books and marketing guru." He and his wife are also the parents of nineteen children, fourteen of whom have been adopted from foreign countries. Another contributor, Tim Ferriss, is characterized as "an accelerated-learning researcher, world traveler, and guest lecturer at Princeton University." He is also said to be fluent in Japanese, Mandarin Chinese, German and Spanish, to hold a title in Chinese kickboxing and a Guinness world record in tango, to have coached more than eighty "world champion athletes" and to be the author of several books. We should all have such talent.

Consistent with the backgrounds of the contributors, about a third (thirty-two per cent) of life-changing books came from the non-fiction self-help genre. That includes those intended to provide inspirational direction, overcome a personal problem, or encourage innovative business practices. Examples include *The 7 Habits of Highly Effective People* by Stephen Covey (cited twice), *Learning to Love Yourself* by Gay Hendricks, *Man's Search for Meaning* by Victor Frankel (also cited twice), etc.

Fiction, both classical and contemporary, ranked second (twenty-two per cent) in the type of books chosen. That included two classic novels, e.g. *Don Quixote, Siddhartha*, and ten contemporary novels, e.g. *The Alchemist, To Kill a Mockingbird, A Tree Grows in Brooklyn*, etc. Clearly the great 19th Century novels of inspiration and devotion didn't do much for these individuals, nor did the great Russian novels of Tolstoy or Dostoyevsky, or those modern classics of Hemingway or Joyce. Readers admired those novels, but they didn't report they were life-changing.

The remaining collection of influential works were drawn from a variety of fields including seven biographies, e.g. *Ghandi, Veeck—As in Wreck: The Chaotic Career of Baseball's Incorrigible Maverick*, Kennedy's *Profiles in Courage*, etc.; general science, e.g. *The Silent World* by Jacques Cousteau, *On Aggression* by Konrad Lorenz, *Psycho-Cybernectics* by Maxwell Maltz etc.; and one each in History (*The Passion of the Western Mind* by Richard Tarnas), mythology (*The Hero with a Thousand Faces* by Joseph Campbell) and politics (*Mein Kampf*). The Bible, the most popular book of all time, was mentioned only once. And in spite of the popularity of contemporary memoirs, only one was cited, *Instant Replay: The Green Bay Diary* by Jerry Kramer.

An overwhelming majority of book-induced effects were changes in a person's beliefs, commitments, or intentions to act. In addition, each such change was usually preceded by a dilemma in the person's life that the book dealt with and offered a solution.

Ten readers described relatively specific changes the book motivated them to undertake including being more sociable or goal directed and, in the case of five individuals, emphasizing the importance of controlling the course of one's life and taking responsibility for one's actions.

I pulled it [Psycho-Cybernetics by Maxwell Maltz] off the shelf, started reading, and found it was easy to read and made a lot of sense. I took the book home and read it cover to cover, and then started again at the beginning. One message stood out for me: You are in control of your destiny. Your mind is very powerful; what you think is your reality. Rudy Ruettiger

Fifteen readers described a wide range of effects including "lightening up," "doing what is right," trusting your instincts or desires, taking risks and being more courageous.

The most frequent effects were spiritual/cognitive changes that were noted by seventeen contributors. Gaining understanding or insight about an event in their life was the most often mentioned (8), followed closely by those who turned toward a more spiritual life (7) with two individuals reporting a book that helped them to "find the real me" or gain a greater sense of their own identity.

I had been trying to control things that were fundamentally uncontrollable and the cost had been the moment-by-moment disruption of my peace of mind. ....But now with the help of Epictetus [The Book of Life] I realized the pointlessness of trying to control my emotions. They have a life of their own, and they will last as long as they last. Applying the wisdom Epictetus conveys in his first sentence, I relaxed my resistance, letting go of my effort to wish my feelings away.......That brief moment in time exerted such a powerful positive influence on me that it has affected the way I live my life and practice my profession ever since. Gay Hendricks

Books That Made the Difference, prepared for the Center for the Book by Gordon and Patricia Sabine constitutes the broadest sample of readers who were asked about a book that changed their life.[61] The Center for the Book in the Library of Congress was established in 1977 to promote the reading of books and improve literary standards in the U.S. In 1983 the Center conducted the "Books That Made the Difference Project" in which over 1,382 individuals were asked to respond to two questions: "What book made the greatest difference in your life?" and "What difference did it make?"

The sample consisted of a group of "interesting Americans" chosen in a thoroughly unsystematic fashion simply because of "who they were, what they'd done, where they worked, sometimes even how they looked or precisely where we [Gordon and Patricia Sabine] found them." The sample consisted of an extraordinarily broad collection of individuals ranging from well-known actors, politicians, writers, and athletes to an unknown airline stewardess, dairy farmer, logger, waitress, and innkeeper.

They were interviewed in twenty-four large American cities and twenty-four smaller ones across the country. The final sample consisted of 200 individuals whose responses were reported in

61 *Books That Made the Difference: What People Told Us.* Gordon and Patricia Sabine, 1983. Hamden, CT: Shoe String Press.

the Sabine's book, *Books That Made the Difference*. Their volume is organized around the difference the book made in the respondent's life. Representative examples of these differences along with the title of the book are shown below:[62]

How much difference do books really make?

The difference that it [The Secret in the Daisy by Carol Grace] made was enormous. It took me from a miserable, unhappy wretch to a joy-full, glad-to-be-alive human. I fell so in love with the book that I searched out and married the girl who wrote it. Walter Matthau

Seeing yourself in print

Before, I always thought I was just some kind of weirdo. With the book [Passages by Gail Sheehy]. it was nice to know everybody else was going through the same thing too.

Books that inspired careers

What made the greatest differences were the plays—and I will not pick out just one—the plays of Bernard Shaw, which resolved me at about the age of fifteen or sixteen that if I could make it, I'd become a playwright. That made the difference of pointing the way I wanted to go and that was the way I went. Clare Boothe Luce

---

62 The Sabine's original list of seventeen differences has been reduced to eleven as six of those differences had only one response or overlapped with one of the eleven that are reported.

Early reading

For some reason, leatherbound copies of the goings-on in Congress lined the shelves of our living room, and I pored over them when I was twelve. I had never read anything so funny. From then on, I knew I wanted to do comedy. Alan Ada

In spite of their limited representativeness, these anecdotal accounts leave little doubt that books can be powerful agents of change for a wide range of individuals. It is also abundantly clear that a multiplicity of books can have this effect—from the *Sears Catalogue* to *Instant Replay: The Green Bay Diary of Jerry Kramer*, *Don Quixote* to Homer's *Odyssey* and Aristotle's *Ethics*. This indicates that whatever influence the experience of reading a book might have, it will be highly personal. In all the accounts I've mentioned rarely was a book cited more than once and those that were number less than ten. The Bible was the one exception. It was cited fifteen times in the Sabine 's volume—the largest and most representative of the samples reported. However, the Bible's impact is not universal, as it was not cited by any of the seventy-one writers who contributed to the Coady & Johannessen volume and only one of the fifty-five individuals interviewed by Canfield and Hendricks.

The wide range in the age at which an influential book is read is also evident from these accounts. Readers recalled books that they read early in their childhood, adolescence and throughout their adult life. In addition, most indicated they were surprised by the book's impact; it was unexpected, more a matter of happenstance than one intentionally planned. In this respect the experience of reading an influential book is much like the process that occurs when any kind of fortuitous event alters behavior.

Empirical Evidence

However, rather than personal testimonials of this sort, I was looking for more general tests of the various hypotheses about the effects of reading literature, tests that would determine how widespread and long lasting such an effect might be compared to the many other ways we attempt to change behavior. I was aware of various theories about the effects of reading literature that date back as far as antiquity, but as far as I could tell, the empirical study of these views under natural reading conditions was virtually non-existent.

It seemed to me then that literary scholars had examined almost everything else about literature except its influence on readers. Robert Wilson put it well: "Although most persons would agree that reading may be generally efficacious in directing an individual's development, few attempts have been made to define its influence more precisely."[63] Perhaps the question is simply too complex or too "psychological" for the critics. They may simply assume that reading literature influences individuals, that, indeed, it sometimes affects their thought and personality but that it is hopelessly naive to expect that empirical studies will ever be able to clarify the nature and extent of its influence.

63 Robert N. Wilson, Literary Experience and Personality. *Journal of Aesthetics and Art Criticism*, 1956, 14, 47-57.

In fairness, writers and critics recognize the importance of the question. In his remarks at the PEN conference, The Power of the Pen, Salman Rushdie acknowledged that, while it is unusual for literature to have a major influence on one's life, occasionally readers will fall in love with a book that changes them permanently. He referred to *Uncle Tom's Cabin* that "changed attitudes toward slavery, and Charles Dicken's portraits of child poverty [that] inspired legal reforms and J.K. Rowling [who] changed the culture of childhood, making millions of boys and girls look forward to 800 page novels." He also noted that occasionally a reader will fall in love with a book that "leaves its essence inside him…and those books become parts of the way we see our lives; we read our lives through them, and their descriptions of the inner and outer worlds become mixed up with ours—they become ours." The experience is rare but when it does take place it exerts a powerful and long lasting hold on the reader.

In one of the first in-depth, albeit not experimental, studies I found on the effects of reading literature, Martha Purdy analyzed the various forms of learning that occur in reading literary fiction.[64] Purdy conducted comprehensive interviews with five regular novel readers. After coding each interview, she found, not surprisingly, that these readers sought out novels for entertainment and escape. But along the way they also collected new factual information, as well as insights about themselves, their personal beliefs, and values. They did not necessary read with the primary intention of learning, but it was an inevitable

64 Martha Leete Purdy. *Adult Experience of Learning from Novels.* Doctor of Education dissertation, Virginia Polytechnic Institute and State University, 1998.

consequence of an incidental learning process that characterizes virtually every experience, including that of reading literature.

My search uncovered several investigations of the use of reading experiences as a therapeutic tool. This approach, known as "bibliotherapy," is the "use of print and non-print material, whether imaginative or informational...to effect changes in emotionally disturbed behavior."[65] While bibliotherapy was employed initially with individuals institutionalized in prison or mental hospitals, it has recently been extended to other community settings, including schools and libraries. All such programs attempt to use the experience of reading written material to change a person's behavior, attitudes or values in some way.

Is bibliotherapy an effective way to change behavior? The behaviorally oriented approaches, during which individuals are asked to read self-help materials in treating problems such as alcoholism, obesity, and social anxiety, appear to be the most successful. But even in these cases the evidence for their effectiveness is mixed. A recent review indicated that it was most effective in the treatment of depression, mild alcohol abuse and anxiety disorders and less successful for smoking cessation and more severe cases of alcohol abuse.[66] In contrast, reading fiction, poetry, or creative non-fiction as a self-help tool appears to have only a modest degree of influence that is most clearly reflected

65 Richard J. Riordan & Linda S. Wilson. Bibliotherapy: Does It Work? *Journal of Counseling and Development*, 1989, 67, 506-508.

66 Jennifer Mains & Forrest Scrogin. The effectiveness of self-administered treatments: A practice friendly review of the research. *Journal of Clinical Psychology*, 2003, 59, 237-246.

in attitude rather than behavioral change. However, the research in this area is not extensive and what has been done is methodologically far from elegant.

I have somewhat similar concerns about the studies reported by Hakemulder in *The Moral Laboratory*.[67] Hakemulder summarizes the results of a large number of investigations on the effects of reading narrative passages on attitudes and moral beliefs. Unfortunately, the studies he describes varied widely in their outcomes with few statistically significant results. Moreover they were carried out in the laboratory under highly reactive test conditions in which the individuals were asked to read specially prepared segments rather than intact works of literature. In my view, research with individuals engaged in natural reading experiences seems far more likely to capture the effects of literature than such artificial laboratory situations.

Consider, for example, recent research on some of the newly emerging programs designed to introduce literature to economically and educationally disadvantaged individuals.[68] Most are based on the interdisciplinary humanities curriculum developed by Earl Shorris, known as the Clemente Course in the Humanities.[69] The eight-month course in poetry, logic, art,

---

67 J. Hakemulder, *The Moral Laboratory: Experiments examining the effects of reading literature on social perception and moral self-concept*, 2000. Amsterdam: John Benjamins Publishing Co.

68 Samuel Freedman. To Fire Up Troubled Students, A Program Turns to the Classics. *New York Times,* August 18, 2004.

69 Maggie Riechers Streetside Socrates. Humanities, May/June 2000, Volume 21/Number 3. http://www.neh.gov/news/humanities/2000-05/clemente.html.

history, and moral philosophy described in Shorris's book *Riches for the Poor* has been adopted at several locations throughout the country, with a goal of fifty such programs in the coming years. According to Shorris, the intensive study of the humanities is an effective way to move people out of poverty and into community engagement and meaningful work.

How successful is the course in achieving this goal? Gathering evidence to answer this question is not easy. It is often difficult to track down participants in the courses, many of whom lead chaotic lives with no permanent addresses or phone numbers. Shorris reports a preliminary evaluation in the Appendix to his first book, *New American Blues: A Journey through Poverty to Democracy* (Norton, 1996). Only half (fifty-five per cent) of the students were able to complete the course the first time he offered it, leaving a sample of seventeen individuals for the pre- and post-course assessment analysis. The findings indicated there were modest gains in the student's self-esteem and use of cognitive strategies. But most of the change scores were not significant, and in the absence of comparative data from a group of individuals who were not able to participate in the course or were enrolled in an alternative program, it is difficult to know what to make of these findings.

Slightly better evidence is available from a class in humanities offered by faculty at Stanford University to groups of fifteen to twenty female addicts and ex-convicts who have been placed in a residential (Hope House) drug and alcohol treatment program. The Clemente-derived course offered at Hope House focuses on classic texts, with an emphasis on political and social issues. Follow-up evidence from the women who have participated in this program revealed that approximately seventy per cent have remained drug free and out of prison, a value that the authors describe as "far better than the national average."[70]

In the tradition of these studies, the Portland-based Oregon Council of Humanities, in collaboration with nearby Reed College, offers a free, two-semester, college level course in the humanities to low-income individuals with limited education. Recently the course was introduced to a group of incarcerated inmates at a medium-security adult male correctional facility in Eastern Oregon. The course, known as Humanity in Perspective (HIP) seeks to provide the knowledge and intellectual skills that can foster significant changes in the lives of the participants. It is based on the conviction that all individuals, no matter what their life histories or economic circumstances, can learn to live better lives once they have the opportunity to explore the great literature and ideas of the past and present. In the Fall semester students read key Ancient Greek works drawn from texts in history (Thucydides), philosophy (Aristotle & Plato), poetry (Tyrtaeus & Sappho), and drama (Sophocles & Euripides). In the Spring Semester readings were selected from more contemporary texts including Emerson, Thoreau, Mark Twain, Flannery O'Connor, Tennessee Williams, Martin Luther King and Toni Morrison.

I was recently given an opportunity to evaluate the course. A

70 Satz, D & Reich, R. *The Liberal Reach: Teaching Humanities to the Poor.* Dissent, Winter 2004. www.susanohanian.org/show_commentary.php?id=242.

questionnaire was developed in order to compare the student's responses both before and after they participated in the course. The survey consisted of three sections designed to assess the impact of the course in a number of areas including literary activities, critical thinking, writing ability and self-esteem. The results in both settings indicated that the course exerted considerable influence on a wide range of student attitudes and beliefs.

The students in Portland displayed a significant improvement in their level of self-esteem, verbal ability, and in their analysis of the major course themes. It also had a positive impact on the inmates who displayed an overall positive change in their literary activity, writings skills, and their treatment of the major course themes. These findings should be tempered somewhat by the fact that the samples were small and there was considerable variation between the students and settings in which the course was offered. For instance, the two groups were not evenly matched, especially in terms of educational background. Unlike the students in Portland, most of the inmates had enrolled in GED and other education courses offered at the institution. As a result, they had recent educational experiences that were directly assessed in the survey, whereas many of the students in Portland had been out of school for several years or had never participated in any non-school educational programs.

The inmates were also highly motivated to enroll in the class, while it was difficult to recruit students for the course in Portland. Class attendance at the prison was required and the inmates were always escorted to the classroom by a guard. In contrast, the students in Portland often had to drive or take the bus a considerable distance to reach the classroom and, on occasion, missed the evening class because of travel or personal constraints. These difficulties may account for the differing course graduation rates between the two groups: the rate for the course in Portland, over its five year history, is forty-one per cent, while in its first year, the students at the prison had a eighty-six per cent graduation rate.

In combination, these differences may explain why the course did not have the same effects in the two settings. That is, gains on one measure by participants in one of the groups were not necessarily associated with comparable gains by the students in the other group. It is evident, however, that the humanities courses in Portland and the correctional institution exerted considerable influence on the students. The overwhelming impression one gets from examining these data is that the experience of reading and discussing some of the great works of literature went a long way toward meeting the educational goals of the Humanity in Perspective Program and fostering a number of significant changes in the lives of the students.

These findings were supported by uniformly positive anecdotal reports by the students in both settings. A student who spoke at the Spring 2006 graduation ceremony in Portland eloquently expressed the students' sentiments:

> My classmates and I answered an invitation to come and learn. Twice a week for two semesters we gathered together to discuss some of history's great

minds and ideas. We read and discussed the Greek Philosophers and dramatists...the foundations of Democracy in America...the Transcendentalists and contemporary writers...issues of slavery, prejudice, women's rights, civil rights, human rights. We wrote papers and formulated thesis arguments. These things alone would constitute an interesting educational experience. But this is not all we learned. We learned that these were not just texts to be read, but ideas to live by. We learned about the power of words to harm or to help. We learned how to listen, and how and when to speak up. We learned that our ideas and our opinions are important. We learned that each of us can make a difference in our lives, in our community, in the world. We learned these things not only from these texts and from our teachers, but from each other.

"Changing Lives Through Literature" is a somewhat similar approach to investigating the question I have posed. It is designed as a sentencing alternative for high-risk offenders with a large number of prior convictions.[71] In addition, the program is restricted to offenders who express a willingness to participate in lieu of a jail sentence. "Changing Lives Through Literature" is based on the belief that criminal offenders can derive considerable benefit from the experience of reading and discussing major works of literature. Robert Waxler, one of its founders, suggests that "...offenders often commit criminal acts because they operate from a value system that gives priority to

---

71 The average number of prior convictions for the first two groups of male participants was 18.4 per person.

emotions and primal instinct, rather than to reason and critical thinking. We need to challenge that single-minded value system by using novels and short stories that unfold the complexity and diversity of character and human consciousness."[72]

Literature, according to Waxler, can achieve that goal by providing individuals with an opportunity to engage in serious reflection and sustained analysis of their behavior. The program involves intensive reading and group discussions of contemporary literature, including works such as Banks' *The Affliction*, Dickey's *Deliverance*, Ellison's *Invisible Man*, Hemingway's *Old Man and the Sea*, London's *Sea Wolf*, Mailer's *An American Dream*, and Morrison's *The Bluest Eye*. The discussion sessions take place every other week for two hours.

In a study of the first four groups of offenders, the recidivism rate of thirty-two men who completed the course was compared with a matched group of forty probationers who were not exposed to any aspect of the program.[73] An analysis of follow up criminal records indicated that only six of the thirty-two men in the reading group (18.8%) were convicted on new charges after completing the program. In the comparison group, eighteen of the forty men (45%), three times more than the reading group, were convicted on new charges during this period.

72 Robert Waxler. *Why Literature?: The Power of Stories*. Online document: http:// www.ed.gov/offices/ OVAE/OCE/ SuccessStories/Part2.htm

73 G. Roger Jarjoura & Susan T. Krumholz. Combining Bibliotherapy and Positive Role Modeling as an Alternative to Incarceration. *Journal of Offender Rehabilitation*, 1998, 28, 127-139.

While these differences are important, it is not entirely clear they can be attributed to the *specific* works that were read or to the reading experience itself, independent of its content. The differences could also be due to the group discussions or the contact the offenders had with each other, as well as the group leader.[74] Moreover, the attempt to match the groups was not successful, as those in the reading group had more prior convictions and were rated as more motivated to "make changes in their lives" than members of the comparison group. Without further tests that ideally should include a control group of offenders who read non-literary materials, these factors cannot be ruled out as possible explanations for the initial findings.

In spite of this uncertainty, the "Changing Lives Through Literature" program impressed me. It sought to measure objectively the effects of a literary reading program. It did so in a formidable setting with a group of individuals who are not often responsive to recidivism reduction techniques. Perhaps the offenders did gain some insight about their own behavior from the readings and discussions after all. As one of the participants reported: "I started to see myself in him [the ship captain in *Sea Wolf*] and I didn't like what I saw."

To be sure, empirical study of this issue faces a number of conceptual and methodological limitations. There is a lack of specificity in knowing what aspect of the reading material is responsible for the observed effects. Further, most of the studies do little more than establish a relationship between exposure to

74 The groups were led by a rotating group of individuals, including a college professor, probation officer, and a judge.

these materials and changes in attitudes or behaviors, leaving open the question of whether the experience *per se* caused these effects. Finally, the research to date has been based on fairly weak designs, without, for example, comparison or control groups required to rule out alternative accounts of the findings.

Reading great works of literature is not often considered among the foremost sources of personal change. However, evidence reviewed in this chapter makes it clear that the experience of reading a book can exert a powerful influence on human thought and action. This is most likely to occur when individuals face a personal problem, when they are primed and searching for a solution. A great many individuals report it was a book that finally pointed them in the direction of one. Yet these encounters were for most part not planned or deliberately induced by an agent of change. This suggests that both practitioners and investigators of the behavior change process may be neglecting the very considerable influence that reading works of literature can have on individuals.

CPSIA information can be obtained at www.ICGtesting.com
Printed in the USA
BVOW070107220312

285722BV00001B/107/P